A
Steward's
Journey
SOLVING THE MONEY MAZE

A
Steward's
Journey
Solving the Money Maze

DON COLEY

ASJ Resources, LLC
Colorado Springs, Colorado

A STEWARD'S JOURNEY
Published by
ASJ Resources, LLC
2730 Stone Creek Road
Colorado Springs, CO 80908

ISBN: 0-9769839-0-7

Jacket Design
Next Communications
6520 Edenvale Blvd, Suite 112
Eden Prairie, MN 55346

Layout/Typesetting
Angela Messinger
Finer Points Productions

Library of Congress Catalog Number: 2005933361

Printed in India at Indira Printers, New Delhi.

To Pam, the best companion I could ever have
for life's journey, you made this possible.

❦

To my friends that helped transform this dream into reality,
thank you! Your encouragement, counsel,
and prayer mean more than I could ever express.

Contents

If you like what you've got, keep on doing what you're
doing. But if the pain of remaining the same has become
so great that change is the only option, get ready for *A
Steward's Journey.*

SECTION ONE: THE RING OF TRUTH

It is hard to isolate our needs when we have the means
to satisfy our wants.

> *The rich rule over the poor, and the borrower
> is servant to the lender.* (Proverbs 22:7)

If our increases in income are followed by equal increases
in our standard of living, we increase the element of risk
in our financial future.

> *In the house of the wise are stores of choice food and oil,
> but a foolish man devours all he has.* (Proverbs 21:20)

If you need more you are poor, no matter how much you
have. If you have enough you are rich, no matter how
much enough is.

> *Whoever loves money never has money enough; whoever
> loves wealth is never satisfied with his income.* (Ecclesiastes 5:10)

The tastiest filet mignon loses its flavor if you're not
at peace with the person across the table.

> Better a little with the fear of the LORD than great wealth
> with turmoil. Better a meal of vegetables where there
> is love than a fattened calf with hatred. (Proverbs 15:16-17)

Surprises can sideswipe our financial security.

> The plans of the diligent lead to profit as surely
> as haste leads to poverty. (Proverbs 21:5)

Buying high and selling low isn't a smart investment
strategy.

> Do not store up for yourselves treasures on earth, where moth
> and rust destroy. . . . But store up for yourselves treasures
> in heaven, where moth and rust do not destroy, and where
> thieves do not break in and steal. (Matthew 6:19-20)

SECTION TWO: A STEWARD'S WORLD

Some people genuinely are God's gifts to the world.
Other people just think they are.

> For who do you know that really knows you, knows
> your heart? And even if they did, is there anything they
> would discover in you that you could take credit for? Isn't
> everything you have and everything you are sheer
> gifts from God? (1 Corinthians 4:7, MSG)

Executing a power of attorney only transfers legal authority for the management of assets. Ownership remains the same.

It will be like a man going on a journey, who called his servants and entrusted his property to them. (Matthew 25:14)

When God gives His vision, He also gives His provision.

The earth is the LORD's, and everything in it, the world, and all who live in it. (Psalm 24:1)

When was the last time you met a truly generous grouch?

You will be made rich in every way so that you can be generous on every occasion. (2 Corinthians 9:11)

Do we really believe our beliefs?

Christ is the one through whom God created everything in heaven and earth. He made the things we see and the things we can't see—kings, kingdoms, rulers, and authorities. Everything has been created through him and for him. (Colossians 1:16, NLT)

Here's the secret to discovering God's will for your life.

The master said, "Well done, my good and faithful servant. You have been faithful in handling this small amount, so now I will give you many more responsibilities. Let's celebrate together!" (Matthew 25:23, NLT)

Section Three: Living More With Less

Money is a spiritual barometer of our heart's
openness to God.

> *Wherever your treasure is, there your heart*
> *and thoughts will be also.* (Matthew 6:21, NLT)

Generosity, not accumulation, is the path to prosperity.

> *A stingy man is eager to get rich, and is unaware*
> *that poverty awaits him.* (Proverbs 28:22)

Excellence is not accidental. Excellence is intentional.

> *But just as you excel in everything—in faith, in speech, in*
> *knowledge, in complete earnestness and in your love for us—see*
> *that you also excel in this grace of giving.* (2 Corinthians 8:7)

Mastering the basics is absolutely essential.

> *A tithe of everything from the land, whether grain from*
> *the soil or fruit from the trees, belongs to the LORD;*
> *it is holy to the LORD.* (Leviticus 27:30)

Any offering of consequence has a price tag.

> *No, I insist on buying it, for I cannot present burnt*
> *offerings to the LORD my God that have cost*
> *me nothing.* (2 Samuel 24:24, NLT)

There are seasons for every church and believer when extraordinary giving is required.

> *So Moses gave the command, and this message*
> *was sent throughout the camp: "Bring no more*
> *materials! You have already given more*
> *than enough."* (Exodus 36:6, NLT)

Live in such a way that thanksgiving follows wherever you've been.

> *Share with God's people who are in need.*
> *Practice hospitality.* (Romans 12:13)

You can't get water from a dry sponge, and gratitude won't flow from a hardened heart.

> *Then Jesus told him this story: "A man loaned*
> *money to two people—five hundred pieces of silver to one*
> *and fifty pieces to the other. But neither of them could*
> *repay him, so he kindly forgave them both, canceling*
> *their debts. Who do you suppose loved him*
> *more after that?"* (Luke 7:41-42, NLT)

It's amazing how many times extraordinary things happen to ordinary people when they seek God's vision and values.

> *God saw all that he had made,*
> *and it was very good.* (Genesis 1:31)

SECTION FOUR: REFLECTIONS ON THE JOURNEY

I can imagine a lot, but I can't imagine enough.
God can do anything, you know—far more than
you could ever imagine or guess or request in your
wildest dreams! (Ephesians 3:20, MSG)

We honor God when we act as He does. God is a giver.
I have set you an example that you should
do as I have done for you. (John 13:15)

Make the permanent your priority.
The Kingdom of Heaven is like a treasure that a man
discovered hidden in a field. In his excitement, he hid it
again and sold everything he owned to get enough money to
buy the field—and to get the treasure, too! (Matthew 13:44, NLT)

Sominex or Serenity? Possessions or Possessors?
Now listen! Today I am giving you a choice between
prosperity and disaster. (Deuteronomy 30:15, NLT)

It ain't over 'til it's over.
There has never been the slightest doubt in my mind
that the God who started this great work in you would keep
at it and bring it to a flourishing finish. (Philippians 1:6, MSG)

INTRODUCTION

The Road Ahead

Given a choice, I'd rather not write this book. Instead, we'd find a comfortable chair in my family room or sit down at your kitchen table, get a fresh cup of coffee, and just talk. There'd be plenty to discuss, since the conversation would be about money: how we use it, abuse it, and the seemingly endless ways it influences almost every area of our lives.

While it isn't possible for us to meet and have a personal discussion, my goal was to write *A Steward's Journey: Solving the Money Maze* in such a way that it maintains a personal and conversational tone and that you will actively respond to what you read. Notice the extended bottom margins of the book's format? They are there for you to journal as you journey. Take notes as you go. In fact, there may be times when your mind will respond to what you read by exploring something from your personal experience. When that happens, feel free to put the book down and follow your thoughts as they respond, whether to a well-known and time-tested proverb or to a new insight that captures your attention. I encourage you to take your time, evaluate, personalize, and incorporate those things that especially *ring true* to you. This isn't a novel written to entertain, a book that can be skimmed as you race from cover to cover. Instead, it's a journey that takes time to complete, a series of thoughts presented in a particular sequence. *A Steward's Journey* seeks to point you to as much insight and understanding as possible on a subject that is the source of countless problems for the majority of us. Money.

Which leads me to a brief explanation of why I've decided to write *A Steward's Journey: Solving the Money Maze* and how it will be presented in the following chapters. You deserve to know my reasons for writing this book and why I'm asking you to invest the next month of your life in what may potentially be the most exciting journey you've ever taken. It can be a positively life-changing month. So here, in a nutshell, are two statements that form the basis of this book.

- A life lived in harmony with the stewardship principles that are presented in the Bible is characterized by satisfaction, fulfillment, and—perhaps unexpectedly—joy.
- A life lived according to the prevailing view in today's culture about money and material possessions is characterized by anxiety, disillusionment, and—all too frequently—tears.

I believe that one of these two statements will, to some extent, describe all who pick up this book and begin *A Steward's Journey*. One or the other will describe *you*. And so, at the very beginning of this journey, I want to ask you this question:

When you think about the role of money and material possessions in your life, would you describe yourself as satisfied, fulfilled, and joyful, or would anxious, empty, and sad be more accurate?

In writing this book I am aware that great pain and frustration are often associated with the subject of money. I am constantly aware—partially because of my own experience—that there are men and women who lay awake in the middle of the night, every night, unable to sleep as their minds race with fear and anxiety.

About money. Their thoughts are filled with questions but no answers. Where will we get the money to pay all these bills? How long can we continue like this? What will I say when the collectors call, *again,* and want to know when to expect payment? Where did the money go? How did we get into this mess? Is this all life has to offer? Does it have to be like this?

There is a statement I heard several years ago that applies here: *Until the pain of remaining the same is greater than the pain of change, there will be no change.* There comes a time when the pressure becomes overwhelming, when the sheer size of the problem becomes so intimidating that we are tempted to think there is no way out. It seems as though there are no answers for the problems that confront us. Wrong!

There are answers and there is hope. We just have to start looking in the right place. To many, it is perhaps the most unlikely place they'd have ever thought to look: the Bible. Maybe you're a person who was raised in a religious home, and you already have several Bibles of your own. Or maybe you've never attended a church and the only Bible you've seen was in the drawer at the Holiday Inn. You wouldn't have the slightest idea where to look for help in the Bible if you did have one. Frankly, for the purposes of taking a Steward's Journey, it doesn't matter which description suits you better. What matters is that those who are looking for more fulfillment, satisfaction, and joy through a more healthy view of money's role in their lives can find these things by taking a Steward's Journey through the following chapters. Are your current view of material possessions and your current money management practices working for you now? No? Then what have you got to lose? You owe it to yourself, and to your family, to explore a new way. Yes, you may need to change some things and, yes, there may be some pain associated with that change. But if you can look ahead to the end of the journey and see satisfaction, contentment, and joy, wouldn't a little pain now be a small price to pay?

This book is written in the hope and expectation that for many, the pain of remaining the same has become too great. With some statistics indicating that over 40 percent of American households spend more than they earn, the problem can't be solved with the passage of time. *Time only makes things worse.* There must be change if things are to get better. There must be change if fulfillment is to replace disillusionment and joy is to dry the tears.

So this book begins with the premise that a change in the way we regard money and possessions is both necessary and desired. But how? What is our road map? Where can we get reliable directions for the journey?

Consider the following questions. Is it reasonable to conclude that the Bible, an authoritative guide to life for hundreds of millions of people for nearly two thousand years, would pay particular attention to those topics it considers most important to us? And if so, can we conclude that topics repeatedly covered in the Bible are topics of great importance and are ones which may be useful? If this sounds reasonable, then consider these facts:

- The Bible makes constant reference to the subject of faith. Throughout its pages we are told of the importance of faith in our lives. In fact, there are almost 250 references on the topic.
- The value of hope can't be overstated. Ask anyone whose life experiences have led them to the place where all hope seemed gone. The subject of hope is referenced nearly 200 times in the pages of the Bible.
- Paul, writing to a church in the ancient city of Corinth, makes this conclusion: "There are three things that will

endure—faith, hope, and love—and the greatest of these is love" (1 Corinthians 13:13, NLT). Paul's conclusion is supported by *more than* 730 Bible references to love.

- Taken together, the topics of faith, hope, and love are mentioned over 1,180 times in the pages of the Bible.
- Now consider this: there are almost *twice as many references to money*, the way we handle it, and the things it buys us, as there are to the combined references of hope, faith, and love. The Bible contains nearly 2,300 such references.

What this tells me is that the Bible considers proper money management to be an essential element of successful living. But we are faced with a strange paradox when looking at how often the Bible speaks on the subject of money and yet how infrequently these principles of stewardship are publicly discussed today. Compared to how often money is discussed in the Bible, the number of times it is the subject of sermons or systematic teaching is relatively low. Many pastors and church leaders are reluctant to address the subject because they are sensitive to the accusation that "all they ever do down at the church is talk about money."

Follow me one more step, please. What I am suggesting here is that these churches, not wanting to be guilty of the charge that the church only cares about money, remain largely silent on the subject. Not wanting to make their congregations anxious about money talk, many of the helpful stewardship principles of biblical money management are left unsaid. Unfortunately, the result of trying to avoid producing anxiety in the congregation is a strange unintended consequence: it produces anxiety in the members of the congregation. Why? Because when the principles of biblical stewardship are not clearly and regularly explained, a vacuum of knowledge is created. And as many of us learned in science classes, nature abhors a vacuum. Something will rush in to fill the void.

In this case, that something is the secular view of money management that can be summed up in a single word: *consume*. From every direction we are told we can have everything and have it *now*. Buy. Get. Spend. More. Better. New. Be the first on your block. Keep up with the Joneses. Fashion, not function, is important. The message reaches into our living rooms from the pages of our newspapers and magazines and the commercials on our televisions. Car radios ensure that we hear it on the way to work, and just in case the power goes out, huge billboards are ever-present to remind us that happiness, self-worth, or whatever, is just one purchase away.

Unfortunately the advertising executives don't tell us that our spending choices have consequences. Consumption has a price tag. When we spend money on one thing, we don't have it to use in other ways. Unless, of course, our choices lead us to spend what we don't have, thanks to MasterCard and Visa! The consequence of these decisions is money siphoned from our paychecks to pay interest charges, allowing us even fewer choices in the future. But I'm getting ahead of myself. This consumption price tag is the subject of the first several chapters.

Just a few more things that I want you to know before we begin the journey. First, this book has been organized into various sections, each designed to build a foundation for those that follow. The first section, chapters 1–6, is in some respects the most important, because each chapter shares some important Bible insights on the subject. Regardless of what you think about the Bible now, the first section of *A Steward's Journey* is intended to let the Bible establish its credentials on the subject of stewardship and money management. It has a lot to say to us. As you read each of these chapters and consider each topic, I invite you to simply ask yourself these two questions: Regardless of my current view of the Bible, does what it says on this subject have the ring of truth? Is it consistent with what I've learned in my own life experience? Then, if it rings true to you, read on. Involve yourself. Challenge what you read but be open to it as you do. Interact. Ask questions. Use the margins to document your journey.

It's time to stretch the legs and I need a fresh cup of coffee, but I have one more thought before we get started. Maybe you've heard the expression: *If you keep doing what you've done, you'll get what you've got.* Nowhere is this more true than in money management. So, if you like what you've got, keep on doing what you've done. But if the pain of remaining the same has become so great that change is the only option, get ready for *A Steward's Journey.* And remember, you take it with God's blessing.

THE JOURNEY STARTS HERE

A steward on a luxury cruise ship is the cabin attendant. The shop steward is a negotiating representative for union members. The meaning of the word *steward* has changed over the years; it's seldom still used to describe a person of great authority and responsibility. The way I'll use the word *steward* in this book is to describe a person of significant authority. It refers to a person *who manages another's property, finances, or other affairs.*

As you begin your journey you should know that when you act in your role of steward, you possess a tremendous amount of authority that needs to be exercised responsibly.

We're all familiar with the term *journey,* but here are a few thoughts for us to keep in mind as we begin. First, a journey takes time. We may have microwave ovens in our kitchens to shorten the cooking cycle and high-speed trains and planes to get us to our destinations more quickly, but we're not yet in the era of *Star*

Trek's transporter room where passage from one place to another is instantaneous. All journeys take time, and a Steward's Journey is no exception. Give yourself time. This book has been written to be read one chapter a day, to give you plenty of time not just to read, but to thoughtfully reflect on and respond to what you discover. There is a section at the end of each chapter called "Reflect & Respond" that provides you with space to do just that.

Here's another thing about journeys. Sometimes our most exciting and memorable ones are those where we end up in unexpected places. Places where, once we arrive, we discover many magnificent things we would have missed had we stayed on the main road. It can be like the journey taken about five thousand years ago by a man named Abram, described in the book of Genesis, who set out on a journey without knowing the destination. He only had the promise that it would be revealed to him as he traveled. A Steward's Journey can be like that. So be ready.

Finally, it goes without saying that the choices we make in life have consequences, but too often we don't make the connection. So as you begin, be aware that one of the goals of this book is to help connect our financial choices to their logical financial consequences. Because if we don't sort these things out correctly in our lives, we can be like the person who spent all his life climbing the ladder of success, only to discover at the top that the ladder was leaning against the wrong building.

SECTION ONE

The Ring of Truth

CHAPTER ONE

Thanks for Nothing

It is hard to isolate our needs when
we have the means to satisfy our wants.

❧

The rich rule over the poor,
and the borrower is servant to the lender.

—PROVERBS 22:7

Sometimes it's easier to share an important principle by telling a story. Imagine that we're standing at the entrance of one of those huge and seemingly endless candy stores at one of the major theme parks like Disneyland. You know the kind. Wooden barrels overflowing with wrapped candy pieces dominate the floor space. Behind the shelf displays, wall mirrors give the illusion that the supply is limitless. Your sweet tooth's craving can easily be satisfied here.

Now imagine two children near the front door. An adult hands each a hundred dollar bill and says, "Buy only what you need." Get the picture? Now think about the chance that these kids will buy "only what they *need*." Do you think they'll come out of the store with a few pieces of their favorite candy and nothing more? Or is it more likely that they'll be carried away by the choices, unable to separate needs from wants, and spend far more than just enough to "meet their needs."

Now imagine another scene. You open an envelope about a pre-approved Visa or MasterCard, and the enclosed letter says something like this: "Because of your good credit rating we are pleased to open your account with an initial spending limit of $10,000." We both know from personal experience that this scene is far from imaginary. It happens all the time. Unlike the adult's instructions to the child in the candy store, however, the accompanying letter never tells you to "spend only what you need." Instead, its message is one of congratulations, convenience, and consumption. *Why wait? Have it now. You deserve it. Earn points on all purchases and get closer to that dream vacation you've always wanted to take.*

We're like the children at the candy store entrance. Only instead of $100 bills, we have tens of thousands of credit dollars to be used at our discretion, courtesy of the finance companies. Our choices aren't limited to candy, but to anything imaginable. Dining room furniture? We'll deliver. The latest clothing fashions? Wear them home. Home theater with surround sound? Installation is included. A new car? Here are the keys.

In light of this, let's consider the question again: "What chance is there that *we* will spend only what we need?" Our response depends on the answer to an even more critical question: How can we isolate our needs when we have the ability to satisfy our wants? Most of us can't. Those who can only do so by exercising

Notes:

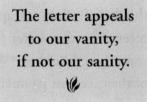

the kind of serious discipline in their spending habits that we'll discuss in chapter 5.

Life is filled with choices. Sometimes we can easily see the consequences of our choices. Other times they're not so obvious. In the consumer-driven culture that is modern America, it has become so easy and accepted to use credit cards to supplement our monthly income that far too few of us stop to think seriously about the consequences of our ever-increasing load of casual consumer debt. These consequences, over time, translate into us having less and less economic freedom and fewer and fewer choices. They include more stress and more sleepless nights. In fact they cause us, as borrowers, to become slaves to credit card companies, as lenders. This means that more and more of the money we earn must be used to pay the growing expenses of our impulsive purchases, now compounded with interest charges.

> The letter appeals to our vanity, if not our sanity.

Let's use an example to illustrate. We purchase a $5,000 home theater system using the store financing service. The annual interest rate is approximately 21% and when you read the fine print a number of potential events can trigger interest rate increases to well over 30%. If we only make the minimum monthly payments on the purchase, how long will it take to pay off the entire account? And what will the eventual price tag be for what first appeared to be a $5,000 purchase? The answers may surprise you.

Notes:

Before we look at the answers, though, it's good to be reminded that credit card companies continue to make their profits only as long as we continue to owe them money. It's to their advantage to extend the time period of our payments as long as possible and they do this by establishing minimum payment schedules in such a way that two things happen.

First, we gain a false sense of what we can afford. We reinforce this belief when we approach the assigned spending limits and receive another letter from the finance company. It usually says something like this: "We are pleased to inform you that, because of the excellent payment record you have maintained with us, we are increasing your available credit." The letter appeals to our vanity, if not to our sanity.

"Congratulations!" we tell ourselves. We must be doing well financially or they wouldn't continue raising our credit limits. Remember the real purpose of the letter though. Their continued profits depend upon our continued spending and indebtedness to them. Remember, too, that although we get the use of the items we bought on credit, we get nothing in return for the interest charges we pay that become their profit. Whatever amount we pay in finance fees is no longer available for us to improve our personal finances.

The second thing that happens as a result of the minimum payment schedule is that we remain indebted to the finance/credit card companies for the longest time possible. After all, if we pay the account in full, they'll have to find another source to maintain

---

Notes:

their profitability, and every business understands that keeping current customers is much more profitable than developing new ones. Once we understand how much sense it makes for the credit card companies to operate this way, we can begin to understand how little sense it makes for us to allow them to continue profiting at our expense.

So how long will it take to pay off the purchase? Much longer than most people think. By making only minimum payments, deliberately set artificially low by the finance companies in order to continue making profits from our interest payments, it can take up to 17 years to pay off the debt. This also means that the price we paid for the system grows as well since we now have to add all of the interest charges to the original price tag. For too many consumers the interest charges add thousands of dollars to the purchase price. I think the truth is that if we really knew how much the system would cost, if it was listed in plain sight on the price tag, we wouldn't buy it because we would know that it is too expensive. To make matters even worse, many of us know that long before the system has been paid for, it may break down and require replacing. Then we're faced with making double payments in order to continue enjoying a home theater system: the first payment to complete the original purchase and the second payment to pay for the replacement system.

> **We live in the ultimate candy store of virtually unlimited consumer choices.**
> ❧

Notes:

We live in the ultimate candy store of virtually unlimited consumer choices. When we start with this reality, then add the ease with which Americans can obtain credit, is it too difficult to predict that serious financial problems are not far away? That personal bankruptcies are soaring? That money is cited as one of the primary reasons for divorce?

Let's look at some statistics. Thirty years ago the per capita consumer debt in America was approximately $600. Some sources say it's now more than ten times that amount and that many American families owe more than $25,000 in consumer credit debt. If yours is one of these families, each year nearly $5,000 of your earnings, more than $400 each month, is used to pay finance charges. That's almost $5,000 every year that could otherwise be spent or invested in things of value for your family. If this is your family, the consequences of your past life choices now limit your current options by $5,000. *Every year!* Actually, the reality is that it will get worse each year as spending continues and debt increases, unless something changes. If you keep making the same kinds of decisions, you are going to keep getting the same kinds of results. I hope that the option of remaining the same is not attractive to you. I'm confident that if you think this through, you'll want to break the cycle of casual consumer debt and establish a strong base for your personal finances. You don't have to be a slave to your lenders, but you do have to want to change.

As you consider whether you want to think and act differently

Notes:

about money, and make wiser money-related decisions in the future, here's another statistic that describes too many modern families. I mentioned earlier that nearly half of American households spend more than they earn in income. Obviously that's not a good long-term foundation for building strong personal finances. It's like the story of the business that took a loss on every item it sold but wanted to make up for it by increasing sales volume. It doesn't work that way! Continuing the old habits only makes things worse, so the sooner you change the better off you'll be. When that happens, you win—but you will also lose. What do you lose? Sleepless nights. Upset stomachs. Unproductive finance charges. Unnecessary arguments with your spouse. Not bad things to lose, really.

What do you gain? Freedom. Choices. Rest. Financial stability. Pretty good things to gain. Really!

One final thought. If you're old enough to have started a Steward's Journey, chances are good that sometime in the past you found yourself in a real candy store where everything looked so good you decided to pig out. Remember what that was like? You got home, sampled everything, and empty candy wrappers or boxes littered the house. How did you feel afterward, when the sheer volume of sugar overwhelmed your body? Not so good? Neither did I. Unfortunately, though, the impact of too much debt is not as immediately obvious as the impact of too much candy. And that makes it more difficult for us to connect our financial choices with their logical consequences so we can identify those

---

Notes:

decisions and behaviors that need to be changed. It's difficult, but not impossible.

Take some time now to review how your spending choices from the past are limiting your current options. Don't hurry here. An honest review of your present financial condition will pay huge dividends as you continue your journey. Use the following Reflect & Respond section to help you respond to what you've just read and apply it to your personal circumstances. When you're done, put the book down and move on with your day's activities. We'll talk again tomorrow.

A Prayer for Your Day

Heavenly Father, You promise wisdom to those who seek it. Give wisdom now, and give it generously. We need to know clearly where we are in order to go where we are supposed to be. Show us how we have made choices in the past and reveal to us the consequences of those choices. Help us understand how our choices have been either wise or foolish. Then give us courage for the journey ahead and confidence that we do not have to remain slaves to consumer debt nor do we need to live in constant anxiety about finances. Thank You that You have a better plan. Amen.

🍂

REFLECT & RESPOND

Casual Consumer Credit Personal Inventory

Indicate which of the following describes your credit card use:

- ○ Balances are paid in full every month.
- ○ We pay the minimum due as indicated in the monthly statement.
- ○ We have outstanding balances on our credit card accounts.
- ○ In the past year we have transferred credit card balances to new accounts in order to reduce interest rates.
- ○ In the past year we have opened new accounts without closing existing ones.

How many consumer credit card accounts do you have and how much do you owe on each? Approximately how much credit card spending did you have last month that won't be paid in full with your next payment?

How much money did you spend last year in interest expenses on these accounts? Reflect on how you could have used this money to benefit you and your family.

Do you agree or disagree that debt can impact our current and future choices and that to some extent we become debts' slave.

CHAPTER TWO

The Peril of the Pyramid

If our increases in income are followed by
equal increases in our standard of living, we increase
the element of risk in our financial future.

❦

In the house of the wise are stores of choice food and oil,
but a foolish man devours all he has.
—PROVERBS 21:20

As goods increase, so do those who consume them.
—ECCLESIASTES 5:11

Suppose, through no fault of his own, a high school student loses his entry-level job at a fast food restaurant. He worked fifteen hours per week during the school year and full-time in the summer. What options are available to this student to replace his income without having a serious negative impact on his lifestyle? Actually, there are quite a few, since fast-food restaurants are seemingly everywhere and they are usually looking for reliable employees. Lack of experience isn't a major factor in getting an entry-level position because most chains have their own training programs. Salary considerations are straightforward because the job responsibilities are usually clearly defined for those jobs at or near minimum wage. Additionally, the student's expenses aren't significant because he is still living with his family and hasn't yet incurred a large amount of fixed monthly payments. With many job openings suitable for this student, it shouldn't be too long before he's working again and his income is back to where it was without much long-term impact.

But what if it were the restaurant manager that lost her job? Or worse, what if the stockholders didn't like the CEO and the board of directors decided to replace him? These situations are more complicated because they involve positions that are higher on the employment pyramid.

The employment pyramid is widest at its base where there are more available jobs in what we know to be lower wage, entry-level positions. Employees are promoted when they gain more experience and become more valuable to their employers, and they move higher up the pyramid. But this upward movement has risks. When a person climbs higher on the employment pyramid, there are fewer and fewer appropriate jobs available. A fast food restaurant may have a few assistant managers and many more employees, but there is only one manager. The chain may have hundreds or thousands of restaurants, but there's only one CEO.

When a person loses his job after climbing higher on the employment pyramid, it complicates the process of finding

Notes:

another suitable position. There are fewer jobs, many more factors to consider, and most of these factors tend to limit options and prolong the amount of time required to replace lost income. If you've ever been in this position, and I have, you'll understand that it can be a very scary place. It can threaten, and cause, significant financial damage, especially if the principle quoted from Proverbs at the start of this chapter has been ignored: "In the house of the wise are stores of choice food and oil, but a foolish man devours all he has" (21:20).

The modern reader may need help in understanding that stores of oil in Solomon's day represented wealth and security. No translation is required to understand the second half of the quote: "a foolish man devours all he has." Yet in a society like ours, one that promotes material consumption and self-indulgence, we find far too many families that have made the choice to devour all they have, and then some. Unfortunately, when they do this, they place themselves in the peril of the pyramid. Living from paycheck to paycheck, they have no "stores of oil" in financial reserve. There is no margin of error, no safety net to catch them in the case of a loss of income or unexpected emergency expenses. Potential disaster lurks just around the corner. Trust me, it's a terrible way to live. Let's spend some time working through the issue and try to identify a better long-term plan for financial security.

First, let me ask this question: How close is this topic to your personal experience? Have you ever thought, *I'm making more money than I ever have; where did it go?* Have you ever commented

Notes:

that your money doesn't seem to slow down when it races through your checking account? Join the club. Your experience supports the second verse listed at the start of this chapter: "As goods increase, so do those who consume them."

Read the following story about the financial situation of a typical young couple. It may be somewhat descriptive of what you've experienced or otherwise know to be true.

Ben and Megan married when they were in college. Both had part-time jobs and money was scarce. Eating out was a luxury, and eating in was no bargain either. Their friends lived in nicer apartments, drove newer cars, and wore better clothes. Yet despite having very little, Ben and Megan got by.

Then came graduation and full-time jobs. Promotions and pay raises followed, as did little Meg, Benjy, and the expensive new world of day care. A condo replaced the apartment and the old clunker was traded in for a flashy SUV. Ben and Megan needed better clothes for work. What had once been luxury was now routine. Ben and Megan had far more income than ever before, but by the end of each month, it seemed they had far less. *What's going on?* they wondered.

We can find the answer to that question by looking at the truth of the verse at the beginning of this chapter. Ben and Megan earned more, and they consumed more. In the words of the reference itself, as their goods increased, Ben and Megan consumed the

---

Notes:

increase in new ways that weren't options to them in their previous circumstances. The new ways could be an endless list of such things as housecleaners, gardeners, car washes, health or fitness club memberships, and many more.

Choices come with increase. Ben and Megan saw their increased income as the perfect way to increase their standard of living. They didn't consider that when they increased their standard of living with each raise, they also increased the element of risk to their financial future. They could buy more, do more, and have more, but in the end they had *less*. They consumed all they had, plus a little extra.

> They could buy more, do more, and have more, but in the end they had *less*.
> ❦

What if one lost a job or the other had health problems that dramatically increased expenses? Or what would happen if any one of a large number of other possible disasters occurred and upset the precarious financial balance of Ben and Megan without their "stores of oil" as a safety net? It would be disastrous.

Sound familiar? I hope that it doesn't, but fear for many of us that it may. The solution to this scenario may seem difficult because our culture screams out to consume all we have. But it really is as simple as this: Make a conscious decision to always spend less than you earn. With each increase in salary, choose to maintain a lower standard of living than you are "entitled to" with your new income. Develop a systematic plan to increase your "stores of oil." Put 5 to 10 percent into some type of savings

Notes:

or low-risk investment account. If possible, take advantage of employer-matched retirement programs. Learn how you can benefit from tax regulations. When you make fiscal responsibility a priority, you minimize the potentially devastating impact that losing a job or being saddled with unexpected expenses can have.

A couple more thoughts and then we're done for the day. Think about the concept of *power*. What is real power? Here's a simple three word definition: *power is alternatives*. The person who has no alternatives has no power. They are *powerless*. The following sports illustration demonstrates the truth of the concept that power is alternatives.

Before major league baseball players formed their union, they played where the owners told them to play and were paid what the owners wanted to give them. Essentially they had no alternatives. There were no other places where they could apply for work with the skills they had. In the absence of any meaningful options, therefore, they had no power.

Then the players formed a union and the power shifted. After a few years the major league players negotiated an agreement that grants them many options. Today they listen to offers from any team and decide where they want to play. In the process, baseball players have created one of the most powerful unions in America.

How does this apply to us? When you or I refuse to consume all that we make and we choose to establish meaningful financial reserves, we gain power. We don't have the same dread of losing a job or accepting less pay to avoid being "downsized" because our

Notes:

financial reserves provide us with viable alternatives. We have the resources to pay our monthly bills until we can find a new position or, perhaps, start a new business.

Spending less than we earn means we create options for ourselves, and when we make that choice, we gain power. In turn, power can negate the impact of fear in our lives, and living with security rather than fear is a goal worthy of sacrifice. Wouldn't you agree?

A Prayer for Your Day

Heavenly Father, changing the way we think about money requires much more than head knowledge. It means that our heart attitudes must be different. So I ask You today to change our heads and our hearts. Change us so radically that money and things will become a source of contentment instead of contention for us. Nothing is too difficult for You, God. Give courage to those who struggle with this and let them know that each day others are praying for them. Thank You that You have a better plan. Amen.

🌿

Notes:

Reflect & Respond

How do you respond to the statement that a foolish man consumes all he has and to the idea of having a standard of living lower than what you could have?

Consider some of the ways you have consumed more as you earned more.

If your family spends more than it earns, where does the extra money come from?

List the extent of your family's "stores of oil," the reserves you have in case of financial emergency. How serious is the risk to your family if you unexpectedly lose income or face extraordinary expenses?

What specific things can you do to create more alternatives that will empower you and protect your financial future?

CHAPTER THREE

The More War

If you need more you are poor,
no matter how much you have. If you have enough
you are rich, no matter how much enough is.

❦

Whoever loves money never has money enough;
whoever loves wealth is never satisfied with his income.
—ECCLESIASTES 5:10

Haven't we all, at one time or another, asked ourselves the question, *How much is enough?* I know I have. One of the times it comes to my mind is whenever another well-known and already wealthy person faces legal problems because they tried to get more. For example, I ask myself why in the world Martha Stewart would risk so much just to gain what turned out to be such an insignificant sum for her: $52,000. Granted, for many of us that's a lot of money. But for her? It was petty cash. It was nothing compared to what she had, and it was certainly nothing compared to what she had to lose.

In the eyes of many, her reputation has been shredded by unflattering descriptions of her as a manager and as a person. Witnesses challenged her truthfulness and character, and this led to a criminal conviction that disqualifies her from serving again in some of her most important past roles. While Martha Stewart retains many loyal supporters, she is just as likely to be thought of as a felon rather than as an entrepreneur or CEO.

When something like this happens, the word *why* seems to scream out for an answer. What possesses someone to risk so much for so little? Didn't she already have enough? It doesn't seem to make any sense.

But we can begin to understand if we refer back to Ecclesiastes 5:10: "Whoever loves money never has money enough; whoever loves wealth is never satisfied with his income." This reference from the Bible gives us some important insight into human behavior, including our own. It says that no matter how much we already have, if we love money we'll never have enough. Since those who love money can never have enough, they'll never be satisfied. And that raises another question in my mind, What good is all the money in the world if it can't bring satisfaction? It's like an itch that can't be scratched and never goes away. How miserable!

Martha Stewart isn't alone. A decade before, this principle was demonstrated by Michael Milliken, a high profile financier who made a fortune selling what came to be known as junk bonds. Milliken, who reportedly made more than $300 million annually when his earnings were at their peak, apparently didn't have enough. His behavior crossed the line that separates legal from criminal and he was convicted of securities fraud, sentenced to prison and a fine of more than $200 million, and barred for life

Notes:

from the finance world he had come to know and dominate. As much as he had, it wasn't enough. Milliken, like Stewart, needed *a little more.*

I know that some of you might be thinking right now, *Those examples are about rich people and I'm far from rich. This doesn't apply to me.* Be careful. The important thing to learn from these examples is not how much Martha and Michael had but how much more they

> **Contentment depends more on *making do* than it does with *making more.***
> 🌿

wanted. And that, unfortunately, is a characteristic that many of us share in common. Never content with what we have, we're always looking for more.

But how much more do we need? Will the next raise be enough? How about a bigger house? a nicer car? designer clothes? country club membership? How much is enough? How much will it take to satisfy us? The answers to these questions are crucial because it's not just the rich and famous who can ruin their lives by putting too much emphasis on money. *Anyone* who loves money never has enough. Please stop and consider the implications of what this means: Chasing after money doesn't result in living a fulfilled life. Contentment depends more on *making do* than it does on *making more.*

Another reference to the futility of always seeking more can be found earlier in the book of Ecclesiastes. Here is what the ancient King Solomon, one of the richest men in human history, had to say:

Notes:

I denied myself nothing my eyes desired; I refused my heart no
pleasure. ...Yet when I surveyed all that my hands had done
and what I had toiled to achieve, everything was meaningless,
a chasing after the wind; nothing was gained under the sun.
(2:10-11)

In an interview with Diane Sawyer on the subject of his movie
The Passion of the Christ, Mel Gibson mirrored Solomon's com-
ments. One of Hollywood's richest and most celebrated stars,
Gibson shared that he'd had it all and done it all, but in the end
it *wasn't enough.* Gibson, like Solomon, discovered that meaning
wouldn't be found in more money.

But the More War rages in ordinary lives, too, and it surfaces
in the practical decisions we make each day. What's the most
active front in your More War? Is it cars? clothes? chocolate? I
often find myself battling along the golf shirt front. I love golf
shirts. They're comfortable, they look good, and they're easy to
care for. The trouble is, I already have enough, I don't need any
more. Then I walk through a pro shop or department store and
something catches my eye. A wrinkle-free-looks-great-on-the-
mannequin golf shirt that seems to scream, *There's room in the
closet for one more, so buy me!* But do I really need one more if I
already have enough? Don't laugh—though the battleground
may vary, each of us fights our own version of the More War,
every single day.

Or how about this? One day I looked in our coat closet and the

Notes:

question came to me, How many people live in this house? two dozen? a hundred? Let's just say that my wife and I are empty nesters, but there were considerably more than two coats hanging there. Weeks later I had the opportunity to share these thoughts with a small group. I asked them this question: If you had a visitor in your home from a poverty-stricken third-world country, and they only had the evidence of what was hanging in your closet, how many people would they say lived in your home? Think about it. Could you easily make the case that there was only enough for your family? Or could a case be made that you had more than your needs indicated? Much more?

I recently read a magazine article about a successful young professional golfer. Unlike other athletes who operate with the financial security provided by guaranteed contracts, golfers must play well each week to earn their income. Theirs is the ultimate world of "What have you done for me lately?" In just a few years, the golfing triumphs described in the article allowed this golfer to move from financial uncertainty to significant material wealth. But the item in the article that caught my attention was this: his new 6,500 square foot home featured seventeen televisions, including three in one room. Seventeen! My guess is that it didn't start out that way. The number probably increased to seventeen. But why stop there? Why not eighteen, or an even twenty? What's the upper limit on *more?*

It's not easy to say no to more. It's not easy to identify needs and commit to a lifestyle that lives with less than could be

---

Notes:

afforded. It's difficult to ignore the barrage of messages from many different sources that all say the same thing: *consume*. But just

> We only gain when we are capable of accepting less.
>
> ❦

look at what the rewards are for exercising this difficult act of self-control. Peace. Satisfaction. Joy. Rest. And consider the lives of those who are never satisfied and always striving. There's no victory to be found in the More War by constantly striving for more; we only gain when we are capable of accepting less.

These are hard issues, I know, and they'll be covered again in later chapters as we continue on *A Steward's Journey* and learn the role, responsibilities, and rewards of the steward. Hang in there. Please.

Two thousand years ago Paul wrote these words from prison to one of the earliest Christian churches in the Greek city of Philippi:

> For I have learned to be content whatever the circumstances.
> I know what it is to be in need, and I know what it is to have
> plenty. I have learned the secret of being content in any and
> every situation, whether well fed or hungry, whether living in
> plenty or in want. (Philippians 4:11-12)

Even though he was a prisoner, I believe that Paul considered himself to be rich because he had *enough*. Compare his attitude with that of too many of us today, who even though we live surrounded by abundance, seem to be prisoners of our need for *even more*. We are poor, no matter how much we have, because all of our possessions do not satisfy us.

It is my hope that by now you've started to evaluate your attitude about money and financial circumstances. Have you learned the secret of being content? Are you rich in what you have, or poor in what you lack? Don't walk away from these questions without honestly wrestling with the answers. Because a lifetime of contentment or contention depends on it.

A Prayer for Your Day

Heavenly Father, help us to find a place of contentment in our lives. Bring us to the place where we understand the futility of always running after more, and where we discover a peace and meaning in our lives that we didn't think possible. Teach us to rest in the sufficiency that You promise to those that trust in Your ways. We're grateful that You are concerned about our journey, and that You promise to guide us in new discoveries. Amen.

❧

Reflect & Respond

Which phrase best describes your attitude about wealth and money?
- ○ We are rich because we have enough.
- ○ We are poor because we are always in need of more.

Reflect on how much would be *enough* for you and your family.

What income levels and/or possessions are you striving for that you believe are critical to your success and fulfillment?

In what areas is it the most difficult for you to curb your spending? What can you do to gain more control in these areas?

Reflect on the things you can do to become more content without increasing your income, possessions, or standard of living and journal your ideas below.

CHAPTER FOUR

Money Can't Buy You Love

The tastiest filet mignon loses its flavor if you're not
at peace with the person across the table.

❦

*Better a little with the fear of the LORD than great wealth
with turmoil. Better a meal of vegetables where there
is love than a fattened calf with hatred.*
—PROVERBS 15:16-17

*Better one handful with tranquillity than two handfuls
with toil and chasing after the wind.*
—ECCLESIASTES 4:6

It's probably better not to confess this but, truth be known, I'm
not a huge fan of peanut butter. Especially on toast, even though
it's an irresistible combination for my wife. I do, on the other
hand, love a good steak. Add a Caesar salad, oven-baked potato,
and hot sourdough bread and you're speaking my language. But
given a choice, I would much prefer a peanut butter sandwich in
an atmosphere of peace and calm than have my favorite meal in

the midst of turmoil. The truth is that with enough money we can afford to buy a great meal, but we can never have enough money to guarantee that we'll enjoy it.

Stop and think about that for a moment. It's possible for us to make enough money to buy the most deliciously prepared meal, but the reality of human nature means that we can never make enough money to ensure it leaves a good taste in our mouth. Yes, money can buy us many things but, like the classic Beatles song says, *money can't buy us love.* So if this is true, why do so many of us act like money *will* buy us love? Why do we work so hard and pay such a high emotional price when the return on our investment is so disappointingly low? Why so many late-night or weekend overtime hours? Do we really need the income from a second job or a second wage-earner income to meet our needs? Have we traded what Ecclesiastes describes as one handful with tranquility for two handfuls with toil and chasing after the wind? These are tremendously important questions because if we don't understand the connection between money and contentment, we will doom ourselves to a lifetime on a treadmill of frustration. We'll get nowhere and be exhausted by the process.

Think back on your own experience. Can you remember a time when your income just wasn't enough to pay your monthly bills? For me it was soon after Pam and I got married and the part-time income of a full-time student didn't give us a very wide range of menu options. We settled for what was cheap and filling. Popcorn for dinner? Sure! The price was right and early in the month

Notes:

it might even have butter! Are you with me? We got very familiar with casseroles made with whatever was in the cupboard at the time. Rice, beans, or macaroni and cheese were served frequently in our first apartments and many days started, or ended, with a bowl of cold cereal. I still remember our first trip to the supermarket when we decided to buy

> **Being *happy* was more important than being *hungry*.**
> 🌿

skim milk long before fat-free became fashionable. Why? It was 20 percent cheaper. An easy decision.

There's something interesting about those memories, though—they're good ones. We don't look back at how deprived we were that we couldn't afford more, we look back at how glad we were just to be together. Being *happy* was more important than being *hungry*, and we valued a good relationship more than a good restaurant. Can you relate? *Better a meal of vegetables where there is love.* We know this is true because it's something we've all encountered personally.

I'm quite sure most if not all of us have also experienced the opposite of this, the point of the second half of the proverb, when money-related conflicts ruined what otherwise would have been a great meal. I think you'll agree with me when I say that it's a lousy place to be, and one to be avoided if at all possible. There's a huge difference, though, in lifestyles that have an occasional "lousy meal" and those that are defined by constant conflict and turmoil. There is no amount of spice and no cut of meat so delicious that

Notes:

it would overcome the bitter taste of a meal ruined by awkward silence. Instead, how much better would it be to regularly season our meals with a generous portion of love-filled laughter? It's a process that begins well before dinner is served, with an understanding of what money can and cannot buy.

The book of Matthew records the following counsel of Jesus:

> It follows that you don't fuss about what's on the table at mealtimes or whether the clothes in your closet are in fashion. There is far more to your life than the food you put in your stomach, more to your outer appearance than the clothes you hang on your body. ... What I'm trying to do here is to get you to relax, to not be so preoccupied with getting, so you can respond to God's giving. People who don't know God and the way he works fuss over these things, but you know both God and how he works. Steep your life in God-reality, God-initiative, God-provisions. Don't worry about missing out. You'll find all your everyday human concerns will be met. (Matthew 6:25,31-33, MSG)

The issue hinges on whether or not Jesus was correct when He said there is far more to life than the food we put in our stomachs. What do you think? From my perspective I don't think it's possible to overestimate the value of a meal shared in peace. Neither is it possible to overstate the destructive force of two lives on a constant collision course with each other.

Notes:

It comes down to this: if we agree with the truth of the proverb at the start of this chapter, and we agree with Jesus' assessment at the end of it, we will establish a vastly different set of personal priorities than if we act on the advice of our consumer-driven culture. What does your experience tell you? What assumptions are the foundation of your life? Is it the meal or the one who shares it with you that is your highest priority?

Like the Continental Divide that is the watershed factor in the ultimate destination of where rivers in the United States drain, our response to Jesus' counsel on this subject forms our own personal watershed. It determines whether people or possessions are more important to us. If our starting point is to constantly strain and toil for the second handful, we will inevitably sacrifice tranquility in our quest to acquire. But if we've learned the concept presented in chapter 3, that we are rich whenever we have enough, we can build our lives on a solid foundation of contentment.

Professional sales trainers emphasize that once the sale has been made it's best to stop selling, and I think I'll take that advice now. The counsel of Scripture is simply too consistent with our life experiences to ignore. What I hope and pray this means to you is that you'll continue on a Steward's Journey and that you won't be willing to accept anything less than the wisdom, purpose, and fulfillment described in these verses:

Has anyone by fussing in front of a mirror ever gotten taller by so much as an inch? All this time and money wasted on

---

Notes:

fashion—do you think it makes that much difference? Instead of looking at the fashions, walk out into the fields and look at the wildflowers. They never primp or shop, but have you ever seen color and design quite like it? The ten best-dressed men and women in the country look shabby alongside them.

If God gives such attention to the appearance of wild-flowers—most of which are never even seen—don't you think he'll attend to you, take pride in you, do his best for you? (Matthew 6:27-30, MSG)

What good is all the money in the world if it can't even bring us a peaceful meal? Is the cost of the newer car or the larger house worth it? Is it worth exchanging a great meal for one cancelled out by harsh words or stony silence? Honestly, where's the sense in that?

A Prayer for Your Day

Heavenly Father, help us to establish the right priorities in our lives. Teach us the real value of money and the true wealth that we have in relationships with those we love. Show us when our desire for money threatens the stability of family. Give us Your mind in this so that we clearly see the impact of our choices. Thank You that You have shown us a better way. Guide us into what is best for us. Amen.

✹

Reflect & Respond

If you were accused of acting like money can buy you love, what evidence could be used to support the case against you?

Are you more or less satisfied with your most important relationships now than you were when you had less material possessions?

Do you think you are "moving in the right direction" in balancing money and relationships, or is it becoming more of a problem for you? Why?

What two or three specific things can you do today to make mealtime more meaningful for you and those around you?

CHAPTER FIVE

Financial Plan or Financial Pain?

Surprises can sideswipe our financial security.

❧

The plans of the diligent lead to profit
as surely as haste leads to poverty.
—PROVERBS 21:5

Suppose one of you wants to build a tower. Will he not first
sit down and estimate the cost to see if he has enough money
to complete it? For if he lays the foundation and is not able
to finish it, everyone who sees it will ridicule him, saying,
"This fellow began to build and was not able to finish."
—LUKE 14:28-30

Has anyone besides me ever started a project, only to discover there wasn't enough money to finish it the way we wanted? Ouch, I thought so! Unfortunately, when these things happen, we not only fail to reach our goals, but the resources spent in the effort are often gone as well. A double loss. The verses above, though, advise us to count the cost before we start and to be diligent in our planning. When we act diligently we'll end up with success instead of failure. Read the verses again. Don't they ring true in your experience?

Nowhere is the expression "aim at nothing and you'll surely hit it" more appropriate than in financial planning, and a key element in any family financial plan is the budget. So today we're going to look at why Proverbs 21:5 makes such a clear distinction between the pathways that lead either to profit or poverty. In the process we'll look at what happens when we begin projects without adequately counting the cost, like the tower builder above. We'll also discuss how developing a personal budget based on income and expenses is such a critical step in the process of becoming a good financial steward and achieving financial freedom. In a sense what we will be doing today is taking a closer look at our own lifestyles and their associated costs. This won't necessarily be an easy thing to do, but it's absolutely essential to ensure that the things we're doing in our personal finances increase our likelihood of success.

Let's begin with two questions:

1. Does your family have a written budget that establishes priorities and guides expenses?
2. Is the budget followed?

Our verses strongly suggest that both questions demand a "yes" answer.

Proverbs 21:5 says that those who act in haste and who do not take the time to plan, end up in poverty. At the same time it

Notes:

describes people who develop a plan as being diligent. One dictionary definition of diligent says what diligence is *not*. Diligence is *not* being careless or negligent. It follows, then, that a diligent person who plans is not likely to be careless or negligent, but is characterized by a careful attention to detail and by his persevering, painstaking efforts.

Another distinction that the proverb draws is the different endings of either profit or poverty. I don't think there's any doubt that if asked to choose between the two, we'd vote for profit over poverty. All of us would. But it takes more than an obvious choice to achieve our financial goals. We need more, we need a plan, and I'd like to explain why the plan needs to be written or it's not a real plan.

First, let's make a very important distinction: plans are more than simply thoughts or intentions. It's not enough to think about what we want to do financially, or have good intentions about how we will manage our financial future. We need to take the additional step of turning our thoughts or intentions into a written plan, and the key part of this plan is the budget.

I once took a class from Dr. Lyle Hillegas, who was then a professor and later the president of Westmont College in Santa Barbara, California. I've never forgotten something he said: "The mark of an educated person is that they can communicate what they think in writing." Obviously this isn't the only characteristic, but follow the reasoning, please. I didn't fully appreciate Dr. Hillegas' comment until much later, when my job required me to use the written word to communicate ideas and concepts with

Notes:

others. It was then that I learned that we really haven't defined what we think until we're forced to convey our thoughts using specific words.

You see, when I write I have to choose each word carefully, to make sure it accurately conveys the meaning I want to share. Often this means I start with some words that are later changed because in the process of writing, I actually come to realize they don't accurately represent what I want to express. In this way budgets are like writing, because in the process of reducing our thoughts about our income and expenses to numbers on paper we are forced to make choices. This process of choosing *how much* we will spend on *what,* and *when* we will do so, is the discipline that identifies our priorities. This is such a crucial point for you to grasp that I'd like you to consider the consequences further. Think about this: an acquaintance of mine explains that "there's a no for every yes." He's right. There are consequences every time we say "yes" with a purchase. Why? Because when we choose to spend money in a specific way, the amount of money we have remaining is reduced, and this limits the choices we can make in the future. When we say yes to a particularly large expense, it results in our having to say no to many smaller options that we would otherwise like to have selected. That's a roundabout way of describing priorities.

> **Without priorities we'll live for the moment at the expense of our future.**
>
> ❧

Notes:

You see, budgets aren't created in a vacuum, they must conform to our real financial circumstances. Unless we wrestle over a written budget and go through the process that identifies our priorities, most of us will not have the discipline it takes to experience the financial success that could be ours. Without priorities we'll live for the moment at the expense of our future. Sacrificing our future in this way could be characterized as a careless and negligent choice. The better decision is the diligent one that understands our financial priorities, because we've taken the time to plan *how* and *when* we will spend our money. *The plans of the diligent lead to profit, as surely as haste leads to poverty.* What an amazingly simple yet wise fifteen word guide for each of us.

A personal budget does more than just establish priorities. It also helps protect us against unwelcome surprises. You know the kind of surprises I'm talking about. Not the fun-filled birthday or retirement party kind, but the how-are-we-going-to-pay-that-unexpected-bill kind. The kind of curveball that life has a way of throwing at us, usually when we can least afford it. Do any of these sound remotely familiar?

"Honey, the washing machine won't drain."

"How many cavities? And he needs braces, too?"

"Well, how much is a new transmission?"

"You backed up the hard drive, right?"

In fact, in the week this chapter of *A Steward's Journey* was written, part of my back tooth broke off and now I need two crowns.

Notes:

Two days later, my computer screen flickered for an hour and faded to permanent black. What pleasant surprises!

Have you ever noticed that it's usually the times when we're already running a little late that the traffic is the worst? Or we're greeted by a road sign that warns: "Caution: highway construction next 10 miles. Expect delays."

Expect delays. The trouble is even though we know that surprises and delays happen, we often don't take them into account when we're making our plans. Their consequences can be severe, but with proper planning we can minimize and manage the impact that a major car repair or emergency dental visit can have on our personal finances.

The goal of this chapter has been to make the case for the need to have a written budget for our family finances. It hasn't been set up as a how-to guide to budgeting. There are other excellent resources already available to help us do that.[1] But there are a few key points about the process of budgeting that I'd like to share before we move on.

First, budgets must be realistic. Another college professor of mine, Dr. Carl Dodrill, said, "The best indicator of what we will do in the future is what we've done in the past." That's been true in my experience, and it strongly suggests that before we devise any spending plan for the future, it's extremely important for us to understand our spending patterns of the past. Major items such as home mortgage or rent, car payments, and utilities are usually well-known and are relatively consistent from month to month.

Notes:

There are other kinds of expenses, however, that we usually don't track as carefully, and the true extent of these expenses may not be easily known. These are categories such as food, entertainment, clothing, and other discretionary items. In the absence of a budget and with credit purchases being so easy to make, these budget categories can easily be much higher than we think. Before you start writing out a budget for the future, look at past bank and credit card statements to determine what was spent, on average, for the past six months. This exercise can be an eye-opener! Often, just the knowledge of how much is being spent on discretionary items will have the effect of helping control future expenses. Also, in instances where expense amounts in newly created budgets are much less than previous spending patterns, it is important to understand how much sacrifice and discipline you will need to keep your spending within budget limits.

Second, budgets must be comprehensive. It's not possible to plan for every eventuality, but it's important to anticipate and plan for all expenses that can reasonably be determined. Avoid surprises and don't be ambushed by budget-busters if you can help it! Be sure to include all of your expenses in each of the following categories:

- Fixed monthly (mortgage/rent, car payments)
- Variable monthly (utilities)
- Fixed annual (real estate taxes)
- Variable annual (car registration, taxes, and so on)
- Discretionary monthly (food, gas, allowance, gifts, and so on)

Notes:

- Discretionary annual (vacation, clothing, and so on)
- Interest charges (this isn't a true line item in the budget, but knowing how much of our income is diverted each month just to service consumer debt often makes us think twice the next time we're ready to make a credit purchase)

Look at where your money has gone in the past and make sure you've accounted for these expenses somewhere in your budget.

Third, budgets must be cash positive. Translation: we can't spend more than we have. For every month that we spend more than we earn it becomes more difficult to arrive at the financial security we want. If your budget isn't cash positive, what can you do to make it so? Revisit your priorities. Eliminate services that aren't essential. Find creative ways to cut expenses where you can. This short-term sacrifice will ultimately be a long-term investment in your future.

Notes:

A Prayer for Your Day

Heavenly Father, help us bring financial discipline into our lives, so that we can rest in the knowledge that we are becoming the stewards You want us to be. Teach us to be diligent, and show us how to be careful with all of our resources. We give You permission to act in us to remove all traces of negligence. Show us ways to earn creatively, spend sparingly, and invest wisely. Cover our efforts with Your favor and assure us that You desire only what is good for us. Be with us and provide courage for the journey to come, and give us the strength to complete it. Thank You that You have a better way. Amen.

❧

REFLECT & RESPOND

Do you have a comprehensive written monthly budget of your income and expenses? How do you regularly compare your actual expenditures with budget estimates? What actions do you take if your expenses exceed estimates?

On a scale of 1 (least diligent) to 10 (most diligent), how would you describe the management of your financial affairs? What can you do to improve?

List the top five financial priorities you have for you and your family. Do your monthly expenses reflect your priorities? What can you do to adjust your spending habits to conform to your stated priorities?

Consider whether you've ignored any "Expect Delays" signs in your household that have you worried about the impact on your budget and monthly finances.

CHAPTER SIX

How Good Is Your Financial Advisor?

Buying high and selling low isn't
a smart investment strategy.

❧

Do not store up for yourselves treasures on earth,
where moth and rust destroy…. But store up for yourselves
treasures in heaven, where moth and rust do not destroy,
and where thieves do not break in and steal.
—MATTHEW 6:19-20

Here's a thought that should cause us to pause and seriously think about why we do some of the things we do. Landfills and junk-yards are littered with the things we once traded for our hard-earned dollars.

You remember, they were the things we just had to have. The convenient things to make our lives easier. The pretty things to make our homes or us look more beautiful. The prestigious things to make us feel more important. All just *things*. Now, all just *junk*.

Depressing when we look at it that way, isn't it? I've found that another way to gain some perspective is to have a garage sale. We set up the tables, sort out the things to sell, and then struggle to set prices. Why is it such a struggle? Maybe it's because we remember what the item was worth to us once, and we're afraid of how little we'll get for it when the bargain hunters descend at dawn. We're faced with the reality that what we once valued at $50 or $500 or anywhere in between, has more than likely depreciated so drastically that it will eventually be given away for pennies on the dollar. We struggle because we know that we'll soon be in the position of selling at a very low price what we once bought for a much higher one.

> **Isn't it amazing how little we are willing to accept sometimes in return for the literal time of our lives?**
>
> ❧

Ouch! Think about it though. When we were buying most of those things, weren't we just responding to the advertising appeals and advice of our consumer-driven culture? Maybe it's time to fire the champions of consumption and get a new financial advisor.

Stop and think. Isn't it amazing how little we are willing to accept sometimes in return for the time of our lives? And I mean the *literal* time of our lives? We have only so many hours in the week to trade for dollars; at work we exchange them to earn a living and meet our expenses. When it comes to spending, then, doesn't it make sense for us to hold out for a better deal? To receive more value? To invest more of our assets—and indirectly our time—in things that give us a better return? Why is it that even

Notes:

though we know it isn't smart to do so, we continue to buy high and sell low?

There is a solution to the money maze, but it's not found in the spend-spend-spend voices of our consumer culture. It's found in the counsel of the Book that says:

- *Don't accumulate treasure that won't last.*
- *The lender rules over the borrower.*
- *The wise create surpluses.*
- *The foolish devour all they have.*
- *Greed is destructive.*
- *Money can't buy contentment.*
- *Planning is critical for success.*

If we think about the points we've discussed in these first six chapters, isn't there an emerging self-evident truth that is confirmed by our own life experiences? Don't they point us to a common sense that is, unfortunately, not all that common?

The Bible's counsel runs counter to our culture's counsel. But the Bible isn't alone in its guidance. There's a fascinating *New York Times* bestseller called *The Millionaire Next Door,* that compares the spending habits of wealthy Americans and those who only have the appearance of wealth. There's a huge difference. I believe the book's research and conclusions solidly support the biblical counsel we've reviewed in this first section. It's especially relevant to this chapter about our buy high, sell low consumer mentality.

The book's authors, Dr. Thomas Stanley and Dr. William Danko, researched the lifestyles of the wealthy and the wannabes,

---

Notes:

and one of their conclusions struck me as being particularly meaningful. As a rule, truly wealthy people tend to apply a different standard when they make purchases and base their decisions more on value than on appearance. Designer labels with inflated price tags aren't their highest priority; receiving a good exchange for their dollar is. Truly wealthy people are more likely to receive better value for their dollars than apparently wealthy people.[1] This difference in approach describes an important part of what it means to be a good steward.

Each of us is different. Our personalities, past history, and present circumstances all combine to make us the people we are and help explain why we are motivated to do the things we do.

Motivations are key. There is no one-size-fits-all rule that covers every person in every situation. The result is that a purchase that is okay for one person may not be for another. Why? Because it's not really *what* we buy that's the real issue here, it's *why* we buy that matters.

Take a look at the following questions. Their answers can give us meaningful insight into our purchasing motivations.

- How important is value to us?
- How much weight do we give to the concept of value when we're considering a purchase?
- How much of a premium are we willing to pay for a designer label that no one sees?
- How much of my car payment is for transportation and how much goes straight into new car depreciation?

Notes:

There's a good chance that these questions will hit uncomfortably close to home for some, but they're questions worth asking. Two people can make the same purchase yet be driven by two widely different motivations. For the real estate agent showing upscale properties, a car represents something more than basic transportation—it's part of how they present themselves to potential clients, and represents an investment in growing their business. Can we agree on that? But the real estate agent is still faced with other value-related questions. A nice car can be an important marketing asset but would it be any less an asset if it were purchased after *someone else* drove it 35,000 miles and paid for the new car depreciation? Probably not.

When we talk about *value*, it's important to understand that it's not the same thing as cheap. Over the years I've learned the hard way that bargain prices aren't necessarily bargains. Is your experience the same? If so, you realize that many factors should be weighed in reaching a decision to buy a particular item. Is it necessary? Will it last? Can I buy it for less if I shop around, or if I'm willing to wait? Are there hidden costs (like interest) that need to be considered? Will its use justify its cost? Here are a few real life examples:

- I hate to buy shoes, so when I do I want them to last. There are shoes in my closet today that have been resoled seven or eight times, but still look great. If only the original purchase price is considered, these shoes were expensive. But when I factor in all the years of service, they've been a bargain.

Notes:

- I can't begin to count the number of times I've bought something just because it had a good price. There's only one problem—I don't always use it! If you don't use something, it's no bargain, it's throwing money away that could be used more productively in other ways. It's certainly not good stewardship.
- Patience pays. The ability to wait for a sale, or check prices at other stores or Internet suppliers, usually means we can get what we want at a lower cost. So what if it takes five days to receive it? How much is our time worth? How much premium are we willing to pay to have something today rather than one week from today? If we're willing to wait we can effectively give ourselves a raise by getting more for our money.

When we refuse to "buy high" we win. When we spend wisely, it shows we value our time more highly. The things we buy will wear out eventually, so doesn't it make sense to minimize our losses by getting the best deals we can?

The verse from Matthew 6:19-20 at the top of this chapter referenced more than just what kind of investments to avoid. It also talked about the kinds of investments that we should make. My summary of the verse is *investments in possessions don't last; investments in people do*. There is nothing quite as satisfying as investing our time, energy, and money in the people around us. Those kinds of investments make a difference and they pay huge dividends. Is there anything more lasting than the memory of a smile

Notes:

on the face of a child we helped? Is there any more meaningful use of money than to invest it in organizations like Teen Challenge and let them use our resources to reclaim and transform lives?

I think the old expression that says you can't take it with you is wrong. There's one thing we can take: people! Our influence lasts beyond our lifetime when we invest in people. Mother Teresa no longer walks this earth, but is she gone? I don't think so. Her work and her influence remain because she invested her treasure in the things that last. We may never be famous like Mother Teresa, or have audiences with kings and presidents like she did, or influence thousands and tens of thousands, but we can make a difference where we are, with what we have. Why not start now? Invest in something that lasts. Invest in people.

A Prayer for Your Day

Heavenly Father, all I have is from You. It is Your money. Help me to spend and invest it wisely. I can't do that by myself. I need Your wisdom to separate my needs from my wants. Give me patience to wait for better value that reflects better stewardship in my life. Guide my buying and supervise my investing. Let me make a difference in lives, see smiles that light the room, and experience the joy of making investments that last forever. Amen.

🌿

REFLECT & RESPOND

Think about the last time you had a garage sale. How did it make you feel to be "selling low?"

How patient are you to "hold out for a better deal" in order to get good value?

On a scale of 1 (not very) to 10 (very), how important is value to you?

How much of a premium are you willing to pay for a designer label that no one sees?

Consider how much of your car payment is for transportation and how much goes straight into new car depreciation.

Reflect on some ways that you can invest more in people.

SECTION TWO

A Steward's World

CHAPTER SEVEN

A Steward's Source

Some people genuinely are God's gifts to the world.
Other people just think they are.

❦

For who do you know that really knows you, knows your heart?
And even if they did, is there anything they would discover
in you that you could take credit for? Isn't everything you have
and everything you are sheer gifts from God?

—1 CORINTHIANS 4:7, MSG

Which are we? Genuine gifts of God, or those who think they
are? There's such a huge difference between the two, and it's such
a vital component of our discussion about what it means to be a
steward, that I'd like us to start this new section by looking at the
question "What makes us the people we are?" Can we honestly
stand up and sing "I did it my way"? Or is there a source beyond
ourselves that plays a defining role in our accomplishments?

Each of us, at birth, was gifted with an innate set of abilities;
we have been uniquely gifted by our Creator. King David described this starting point in Psalm 139:13-14: "You made all the
delicate, inner parts of my body and knit me together in my

mother's womb. Thank you for making me so wonderfully complex! Your workmanship is marvelous—and how well I know it" (NLT). This is a very important understanding for us to have and confession for us to make. It's central to our understanding that we are stewards, not owners, of what our Creator has given to us.

Have you ever met people who acted as if they were God's gift to the world? It may have been the athletically-gifted three-sport letterman in high school. Or the drop-dead gorgeous cheerleader/homecoming queen. Or the self-made businessman who loudly boasts that no one helped him get where he is,

> **If you're all wrapped up in yourself, you're overdressed.**
> ❧

he bootstrapped his way to success. Or the incredibly talented musician or singer who can hear things the rest of us can't, and captivates us by her ability to hit the high notes so precisely. Maybe you've either read about a celebrity that answered to no one or you've lived next door to a neighbor who was "stuck on himself." We've all known people like those described by the saying, "If you're all wrapped up in yourself, you're overdressed." Now let me ask you this: How do you feel when you encounter them? Are they the type of people you can't wait to see again, or would you just as soon avoid them if at all possible?

Now I'd like you to imagine other people from your past. Maybe they had just as much talent and ability as those we just described, but they were clearly different. Ego wasn't a word that anyone would use to describe them. Humble was. Extraordinarily

Notes:

gifted, they possessed a quality that attracted others, not repelled them. We're comfortable with them. They're the kind of people we enjoy because they are not self-absorbed. Instead, they are quick to deflect praise to others or to acknowledge their own contributions modestly and graciously. I know which type of person I'd rather spend time with, how about you?

Doesn't the verse at the start of this chapter sum it all up pretty well? Isn't everything we *have* and everything we *are* a sheer gift from God? And if so, what room is there for us to boast in our accomplishments? How can we act as if we—not God—are the owners of those possessions He has entrusted to us? As stewards we have the responsibility to take full advantage of what He has given us. It is up to us to invest the talent that He gives us, and the reward given to the faithful steward described in Matthew 25:15-23 will become available to us.

There's another excellent story, largely unknown, that describes God's role in making us the way we are. It's found in the Old Testament book of Exodus, chapters 35 and 36. Don't let the funny-sounding names throw you, just focus on the description of how the Creator equips us.

> The LORD has filled Bezalel with the Spirit of God, giving
> him great wisdom, intelligence, and skill in all kinds of crafts.
> He is able to create beautiful objects from gold, silver, and
> bronze. He is skilled in cutting and setting gemstones and in
> carving wood. In fact, he has every necessary skill. And the

Notes:

LORD has given both him and Oholiab son of Ahisamach, of
the tribe of Dan, the ability to teach their skills to others.
Bezalel, Oholiab, and the other craftsmen whom the LORD
has gifted with wisdom, skill, and intelligence will construct
and furnish the Tabernacle, just as the LORD has commanded.
So Moses told Bezalel and Oholiab to begin the work, along
with all those who were specially gifted by the LORD. (Exodus
35:31-34; 36:1-2, NLT)

The Lord gave wisdom, skill, and intelligence to Bezalel, Oholiab, and all those who were specially gifted by God. Further, they
were given an ability to teach that positively influenced others.
The Bible message is clear: They may have been acting like general contractors on this construction project, but neither Bezalel
or Oholiab would have been right in claiming credit for their talents. No, they were beneficiaries of the gifts from God. Moses
reminded ancient Israel of this same truth in Deuteronomy 8:17-
18: "You may say to yourself, 'My power and the strength of my
hands have produced this wealth for me!' But remember the
LORD your God, for it is he who gives you the ability to produce
wealth." That reminder is still valid today.

Bezalel and Oholiab were skilled craftsmen. Why? Because of
God's equipping them. They were able to teach others. Why?
God gave them the talent to do so. Each one of us in our own
way shares the same heritage as Bezalel and Oholiab, and all
those who heard Moses' reminder. Each of us, in our own way, is

Notes:

gifted by God and given the charge to be good stewards of those gifts.

Rick Warren begins his best-selling book *The Purpose Driven Life* by stating, "It's not about you."[1] The steward understands this, because they know that everything begins with God. They know that the pianist's fingers, the singer's voice, the pitcher's arm, the professor's mental capacity, the preacher's message, and the executive's judgment are all rooted in how each one of us is gifted by God. It's a constantly humbling concept, and one that grows in us a new heart attitude—an attitude of gratitude. We need to be reminded of this and live our lives graciously and gratefully. If we don't, it is so easy to become self-absorbed, arrogant, offensive, and miss God's greater purpose for our lives.

> What each person is given is not as important as what each person does with what they are given. ❦

Stewards also understand their responsibility to develop the gifts and talents that God has entrusted to their care. What each person is given is not as important as what each person does with what they are given. That is the essence of stewardship. If we are diligent we can expand the influence of our talents, but there are limits to what hard work can do. All the practice in the world won't transform me into a singer and, at an inch short of six feet, I'll never be an NBA center.

Modern-day Bezalels and Oholiabs amaze me, because God

Notes:

didn't include the skills of the craftsmen when He designed me. My handyman talents are fairly limited to knowing which end of the plunger to hold. Yet He didn't leave me empty-handed. He's gifted me, and He's gifted you. Now it's up to us to be good stewards and to handle His gifts faithfully.

The staggering truth is that each one of us has the potential to be a genuine gift of God to those around us, once we realize His role in our lives and acknowledge His ownership of our talents. That's what a steward is: someone who understands God's role in making us the way we are, and someone who doesn't hold on to the ownership of their own talents. Instead, they are content to manage and maximize the gifts they've been given, on behalf of the One who gave, in order to truly become a gift from God.

That's where it all starts. It doesn't begin with our looks, voices, homes, cars, vocations, bank accounts, or any of our possessions. Those are all external to us. No, it starts on the inside. Stewards begin with an attitude of gratitude that encompasses everything they are or ever will be. They have a realization that each of us is the way we are for a purpose, and our purpose involves managing and maximizing our God-given gifts. We are stewards acting on His behalf.

As we finish today, let's look at the choices we face. We can choose to take all the credit for who we are. We can do it our way. Or we can accept the lesson of Bezalel and Oholiab and acknowledge that our role is to be a steward. Think about it, and tomorrow we'll continue with a longer discussion of what this role means.

Notes:

A Prayer for Your Day

Heavenly Father, take us out of our hurried routines, slow us down, and show us how many talents You've placed in each of us. Give us Your vision of what these talents can become if we will be faithful stewards of them. Please transform us into genuine gifts for Your world. Bring us to real understanding that the world would be a better place if we acknowledged that every-thing we have and everything we are is a sheer gift from You. Thank You for this gift, and help us keep in mind that the credit belongs to You. Amen.

✤

REFLECT & RESPOND

Make a list of your talents and capabilities or, said another way, how has God uniquely gifted you?

How good of a steward are you of your gifts?

What things can you do to be more of a genuine gift to those around you?

If you don't do so already, every day for the next week, consider thanking God for making you exactly the way He has.

Describe how you feel when you encounter people who act as if they are "God's gift to the world."

Describe how you feel when you encounter those who genuinely are God's gift to the world.

CHAPTER EIGHT

A Steward's Role

Executing a power of attorney only transfers
legal authority for the management of assets.
Ownership remains the same.

🌿

*It will be like a man going on a journey, who called
his servants and entrusted his property to them.*
—MATTHEW 25:14

Jesus was a master storyteller. It's amazing how often and how
well He used the simple things that happen in normal life in
order to relate important spiritual truths to His listeners. They
were able to connect to what He was saying because the context
of the story captured them, and involved them with the point He
wanted to make. Matthew relates just such a story, told about
three different individuals who were entrusted with a portion of
their master's estate while he was off on a journey. I'd like to capture the truth of what Jesus said, but convey it in a twenty-first
century context that may be easier for us to understand. The
modern version is about a father, his son, and the terrible disease
called Alzheimer's.

The father called his son on the phone and asked him to come by the house. "We need to talk about my financial affairs," the father said, "I need your help."

The subject didn't come as a surprise to the son, for prior to the phone call the family had received the doctor's diagnosis: Alzheimer's. They watched and waited, fearful of what the disease could do as it increased its hold on a once mentally alert and physically powerful man. Fortunately, though, at this point the father still retained a grasp on what needed to be done, and when his son visited, they sat at the kitchen table surrounded by boxes of financial records.

The father explained what he needed. "Soon I'll be off on a journey and won't be able to get back to take care of my finances. All these records are in order. I've met with a lawyer and signed a power of attorney that gives you legal authority to act on my behalf. Here are my bank records and cancelled checks so you can see how my money has been spent in the past. This envelope has a list of all my monthly bills and when they are due. The box over there has insurance records and the documents for my retirement income. It has all the details of my investment accounts. I need you to manage my financial affairs."

It wasn't an easy conversation but it continued for hours as the two men talked about the future and remembered the past until both were exhausted. Neither man welcomed the impending journey but each knew it couldn't be avoided.

Notes:

For a short while, the father continued to live at home, but soon that was not possible, and he moved to a facility where it was easier to meet his increasing needs for extended care. Then he slowly retreated into the shadows, to an existence that didn't permit communication. There he stayed.

Each month, the son opened his father's records and made sure the obligations were paid. At first these included donations to the church that his dad had attended and served all of his life. The check amounts matched those last written by the father, reflecting an almost lifelong commitment to giving a tithe of at least 10 percent to God's work. Gradually church attendance became less frequent and finally impossible, and the checks to the church declined and then stopped. "Dad doesn't attend any longer," the son reasoned, "and I need to maintain the value of the estate in case it's needed for Dad's care." In truth, though, there was more than enough monthly income to meet his father's needs. The true reason why the checks grew smaller and then stopped altogether was that over time, the son had mentally transferred ownership of his father's assets into the family's account. Since generous donations to church work were foreign to the son's own financial habits, he considered them unnecessary now that the father no longer was able to derive any benefit from them.

Then the unimaginable happened. A cure was found! One that not only halted Alzheimer's but rolled back its effects. The father recovered and returned from his journey with many

Notes:

tears and great celebration. Then he placed another phone call to his son.

"Thanks for your help, Son, but now that I'm well I can manage my own affairs again. Please bring the records by so I can assume the responsibility again." In a few days, as the father reviewed the records and prepared to make his monthly payments, he was saddened by what he saw.

"Son," he said, "you knew that the tithe to the church was the first check I wrote each month. It was that important to me. I've always wanted to return a portion of God's blessings to Him, for His work. Why did you withhold something that was so close to my heart? I trusted you to act on my behalf, to act as you knew I would act if I were still able, but you did not. I'm disappointed, and sorry that I'll have to find someone else in the future to manage my affairs."

Where did the son go wrong? Over time he came to the mistaken conclusion that his father's power of attorney transferred title of the assets instead of merely granting authority to manage them on behalf of his father. Most of us are rather like the son when it comes to our stewardship of the resources that God has entrusted to us. Over time we may come to view them as our own. Our priorities are not the same as our Father's and therefore we withhold spending on those things that are close to the heart of God. That's not an easy thing to consider, but it is the essence of Jesus' story that we read in the book of Matthew.

Notes:

In that story, Jesus described a master, about to embark on a journey. For us today, who are able to fly halfway around the world in a single day, the journey that Jesus describes is hard to comprehend. The first century journey was long and difficult and isolated. To be away from his affairs while he journeyed, the first century master needed people that he could trust to stay behind and manage his affairs. There were no cell phones, e-mail, or Internet cafes for instant communication. The master had only those whom he trusted to carry out his instructions and intentions in his absence. His success or failure rested on their decisions and their continued faithfulness.

> The master had only those whom he trusted to carry out his instructions and intentions in his absence.
> ❦

If you're unfamiliar with this story known as the parable of the talents, it's found in Matthew 25:14-30. There you'll see that Jesus commended two of the three stewards, those who acted responsibly. The third didn't fare so well. To summarize, each of the three was entrusted by the master with some of his assets. He gave five talents to the first, two talents to the second, and one to the third. While he was away the first two stewards invested what they were given and each doubled the original amount. The third steward did nothing. Both his reasoning for inaction and Jesus' condemnation are very insightful to us today. Pay close attention to the exchange between Jesus and the third steward:

Notes:

Then the servant with the one bag of gold came and said, "Sir, I know you are a hard man, harvesting crops you didn't plant and gathering crops you didn't cultivate. I was afraid I would lose your money, so I hid it in the earth and here it is."

But the master replied, "You wicked and lazy servant! You think I'm a hard man, do you, harvesting crops I didn't plant and gathering crops I didn't cultivate? Well, you should at least have put my money into the bank so I could have some interest. Take the money from this servant and give it to the one with the ten bags of gold. To those who use well what they are given, even more will be given, and they will have an abundance. But from those who are unfaithful, even what little they have will be taken away." (Matthew 25:24-29, NLT)

Those are harsh words! Wicked. Lazy. Unfaithful. Words that I don't want describing me! Worse, the master didn't stop with words. He also stripped the unfaithful steward of the little he'd been given, transferring it instead to the one who had been faithful.

Was the master overreacting? Or did the last steward deserve his fate? What can we learn from this so we can understand and act responsibly in our role as stewards?

The exchange clearly shows that the unfaithful steward understood how the master would act, but deliberately chose not to follow his master's example. Instead he was motivated by fear and did nothing. When Jesus called our attention to the master's judgment He showed us that stewards don't have the right to manage their

Notes:

masters' assets the way the steward would like. Instead, it's the role of the steward to understand the master so completely that they choose the things their master would do if he were present.

In chapter 12, A Steward's Reward, we'll take a more in-depth look at the rewards and judgments of the three stewards. For now let's summarize what the proper role of the steward is.

- The steward understands that something entrusted to his care does not transfer ownership. The master retains all ownership rights; the steward's role is simply one of managing those assets for the benefit of the master.
- To fulfill the steward's role we must seek to understand the motivations and activities of the master. In the example of the son with power of attorney, this means reviewing all of the financial documents to see how his father had used his income when he was able. Once the review was complete, the role of the son was to act in the exact same way his father would have acted, if his father had the continued capacity to do so.
- The biblical steward of today has a similar role: to research how the God described in the Bible has committed His resources in the past, and then invest those resources in his care in a similar way.

It's apparent, then, that the role of the steward is to act on behalf of the master. It's not our right to assume ownership of resources that aren't ours. They've only been entrusted to our care temporarily. What an awesome privilege this is, to experience

Notes:

God's trust and to share His work. On our Steward's Journey, whether today, next week, or a few miles down the road, I pray that we will understand what is required of us, and will respond so well that the judgment we will hear in the future will be "Well done."

A Prayer for Your Day

Heavenly Father, ownership is everything. We pray that You will teach us how to regard the possessions we have as Yours, as precious gifts entrusted to our care for a while. Then show us those things that are important to You. Show us Your heart and Your compassion for this world, and how You would involve us to help meet the needs that surround us. Give us the courage to face this challenge straight on. These things are foreign to us, God, but You can make them understandable and make them a place of rest and comfort for us. Shine Your light brightly on the unknown that lies ahead, and reveal Your truth unmistakably. We thank You that Your truth is the way for us, and that Your way is better. Amen.

❦

REFLECT & RESPOND

On a scale of 1 (owner) to 10 (manager), what number do you think best describes your handling of financial resources?

What things can you do to be more faithful in the little things God has entrusted to you?

Think about how knowing God better can make you a better steward. What changes can you make in your life that will let you know Him better?

If you were given a stewardship "performance review" today, would you hear "Well done, good and faithful steward," or would your judgment be more harsh?

CHAPTER NINE

A Steward's Resources

When God gives His vision, He also gives His provision.

❧

The earth is the LORD's, and everything in it,
the world, and all who live in it.

—PSALMS 24:1

Every family that's ever taken a long trip in the car knows that the most common question is "Are we almost there yet?" We get tired and we're ready to *be there*. A Steward's Journey can be like that, too, if we're not careful. So in this chapter (and again in chapter 21), I'd like to take a little time off from the main journey, pull over at a scenic rest stop, and admire the surroundings. My hope is not just to *inform* you about what God *can* do for us but also to *inspire* you about what He *is doing* in the lives of modern day stewards.

For starters, there's the amazing story of a new Teen Challenge facility in San Diego. I think it's a perfect example for today's subject: God giving a vision for something, then bringing the provision needed to convert it into reality. The San Diego staff calls their story the Miracle on 54th Street. Teen Challenge is part of a nationwide network that comprises the most successful drug and alcohol rehabilitation program in the United States. (To learn more about the Teen Challenge program, check out their Web site at www.teenchallenge.com).

The story begins in 1996, with a derelict old building that had once been a 26,000-square-foot medical office complex. Everything of value in the building, located in a high crime area, had been looted. It was tagged with distinctive gang graffiti, and addicts used the abandoned hallways to smoke, sniff, or inject drugs and destruction into their bodies. The atmosphere was like the thief that the Bible says "is only there to steal and kill and destroy" (John 10:10, MSG).

> The building had once been a place of healing and then became a place of death. But God wouldn't let it stay that way.
> 🌾

Here's what a member of the board of directors thought at the time:

"The building looked like something in a war zone. All the glass was broken. Anything that could be ripped out and stolen was gone, including some of the electrical wiring. The place was filthy and water damaged. I had some real misgivings about what I was undertaking. All of my career experience said this would be a disaster. The amount of money that would be required would be so far above our present fund-raising history that it would surely fail."[1]

That's not a very encouraging picture, is it? But God had another vision for the facility, and it is described this way in John 10:10: "My purpose is to give life in all its fullness" (NLT). As this

Notes:

is written, after eight years of miraculous faith-building provision, His purpose is being accomplished through Teen Challenge. How it happened would take too long to recount, but here are some of the highlights:

- Hundreds of thousands of dollars were raised in a few months to make the down payment.
- An architect designed the facility conversion, drew plans, and helped negotiate the city's bureaucratic maze—at no charge.
- Hundreds of volunteer laborers from throughout the United States came at their own expense and donated nearly half a million dollars in labor.
- When city officials insisted on installation of a budget-busting commercial grade fire sprinkler system, a local businessman became aware of Teen Challenge through a fund-raising golf tournament. He arranged to tour the facility, heard about the need, and immediately wrote out a check for $75,000.
- A start-up business, eager for the opportunity to promote its new venture, arranged for an army of volunteer construction workers to complete the men's locker room and showers, a library, exterior landscaping, and painting. In a single day more than 100 tradesmen completed the job, at no cost to Teen Challenge for either labor or materials!
- Severe shortages of drywall caused prices to skyrocket, material costs more than doubled, and work could not be scheduled. Less than a week later, the supplier called back.

Notes:

It seems there had been an accident; a truck overturned and damaged a load of drywall. Teen Challenge could have it simply by providing a truck and labor to haul it away. The salvaged amount was just enough to complete the job.

- Ceramic floor tiles were donated and then installed by experienced workers that happened to be part of the Teen Challenge program at just the right time.
- A dropped acoustic tile ceiling was needed to complete the chapel. Again, just at the right time, the father of a Teen Challenge student donated all materials and installed it with the help of his son. It seemed a small price to pay for the help his son received.
- Carpet for the chapel was provided by a church whose pastor had graduated from a Teen Challenge program twenty years earlier.[2]

Eight years after the Teen Challenge board member thought that disaster would be the most likely outcome, he joined five hundred other supporters as they dedicated the new facility, completely renovated and debt free. When those present were told that the building was finished but it was not yet furnished, they responded with gifts that were more than enough to complete the job.

I like this story not just because it demonstrates how God makes provision when He gives a vision, but because it mirrors real life. This was a building that had once been a place of healing, and then became a place of death, but God wouldn't let it stay that way. He had a plan for more. *My purpose is to give life in all*

Notes:

its fullness. His purpose is being fulfilled in the Miracle on 54th Street, and families are regaining their sons, husbands, and fathers. (Other Teen Challenge facilities specialize in helping women regain productive lives.)

That's not the only story of God's provision. Here's another about a boy, not even ten years old. He was only seven when he was challenged, along with his young friends at church, to help raise money to tell other kids about God. Even though he was only seven, he pledged to raise $1,000. Would you be surprised if I told you that, when all was said and done, when he'd written letters, made phone calls, and shared his story, this one boy was responsible for raising $1,200? What if I told you that he was so encouraged by God's provision that the next year, when he was all of eight years old, he pledged to raise $3,000? Because of his efforts, when the final totals were counted that year, almost $3,100 was given to share the good news. So what does a faith-filled nine-year-old do when it's time to make a difference the next year? Would you believe he pledged to raise $5,000? And would you also believe that in the third year God ended up directing more than $7,000 into ministry through the efforts of this single boy? Believe it! In three years one elementary-school student, with no visible means to do so, was responsible for investing more than $11,000 in telling other boys and girls about God.[3] Why? If you ask him, he'd say it was what he thought God wanted him to do—it was God's vision. And God's provision always follows His vision.

I've got one more story to share before we finish for the day,

Notes:

but first I want to establish the principle at work here. Nearly at the end of His life on earth, Jesus gave His followers a vision for what He wanted them to do: "Go out and train everyone you meet, far and near, in this way of life, marking them by baptism in the threefold name: Father, Son, and Holy Spirit. Then instruct them in the practice of all I have commanded you" (Matthew 28:19-20, MSG). Reduced to a single word, He said "Go." That was the vision He left to His followers. But although He told them to go, He knew that something critical was missing. We can find His instruction for what was missing in the beginning of the book of Acts: "Do not leave Jerusalem until the Father sends you what he promised. Remember, I have told you about this before.... But when the Holy Spirit has come upon you, you will receive power and will tell people about me everywhere—in Jerusalem, throughout Judea, in Samaria, and to the ends of the earth" (1:4,8, NLT). You might say that after He told His followers to go, He then told them to "Stay." They needed to stay in Jerusalem until they had received the provision that would empower them to accomplish the vision.

I'm a father, and far from a perfect one. But I know that no father can justifiably give their children something to do—let's call it a vision—that they're not equipped to handle. Here's how Luke describes this principle:

> This is not a cat-and-mouse, hide-and-seek game we're in. If
> your little boy asks for a serving of fish, do you scare him with a

Notes:

live snake on his plate? If your little girl asks for an egg, do you trick her with a spider? As bad as you are, you wouldn't think of such a thing—you're at least decent to your own children. And don't you think the Father who conceived you in love will give the Holy Spirit when you ask him? (11:10-13, MSG)

Apart from divine provision, there is no plausible explanation for our story of what one small boy could do when he believed God's vision, or what hundreds could accomplish in San Diego to reclaim a broken building and restore battered lives. Yet God promises His provision to us when we see His vision, believe it, and are willing to be used by Him.

The reference at the beginning of this chapter says "the earth is the LORD's, and everything in it, the world, and all who live in it." Everything means everything, including the land and the harvest it produces.

We can catch a glimpse of this principle at work in a story of extraordinary provision in the harvest of one crop in the Pacific Northwest. A young couple prayed about what God wanted them to do in response to His vision of ministry for their church. They sensed He wanted them to be very generous and make a significant gift to help make the vision become a reality. The couple grew asparagus on their farm. As harvest time grew near, it was obvious that something unusual was happening. It took the laborers much longer than expected to complete their work, so great was the harvest that year. In fact, it was big enough to satisfy all of the

Notes:

commitment that the couple had made. Now, before we attribute the abundance to "a good year," consider this: none of the surrounding farmers experienced similar results. The adjacent farms all had the kind of crops that would have been expected in a normal year.

Coincidence or provision? That's up to each of us to decide. But as we look at the world and everything in it—including ourselves—let's be open to the reality that God wants to accomplish His purpose and His provision through us. Stewards are not limited to their own resources; they have access to the unlimited resources of the One who has everything. For the steward that's an exciting thought, and an awesome place to be.

A Prayer for Your Day

Heavenly Father, I am glad to thank You for all that you do. Thank You for not calling us to do anything You don't equip us to do. Thank You for sending Your provision to those who faithfully follow Your direction. Thank You for the testimonies in this chapter. Make my life one of these testimonies. Teach me the truth of how You want to provide for me and through me to meet the needs all around me. Amen.

☙

REFLECT & RESPOND

Has anyone ever shared personally with you about how God miraculously provided for them? How do you feel when you hear real-life stories of God's provision?

Do you know a person or organization that is waiting on God's provision? Consider how your financial gifts can be part of the answer to their prayers.

What would it be worth to you to see God provide miraculously in the life of someone you know?

Think about visiting a Teen Challenge center, Salvation Army facility, or Christ-centered homeless shelter or food bank and ask them about instances where God has given the provision for their vision.

CHAPTER TEN

A Steward's Responsibility

When was the last time you met a truly generous grouch?

❦

You will be made rich in every way so that
you can be generous on every occasion.
—2 CORINTHIANS 9:11

I don't know about you, but there are some words that feel good to me. Newborn. Rainbow. Hawaii. Chocolate. They're like my favorite shirt—the well-worn one my wife wants to throw out when I'm not looking. They just fit comfortably and wear well. Generosity is a word like that. Only unlike calorie-laden chocolate, I can't think of anything negative about generosity.

For just a moment I'd like us to imagine what it would be like to live in a community that could be described in a single word: generous. It's a place where yes is heard more often than no, and where selfishness seems oddly out of place. When there's a need, there are more than enough people to fill it. Time is not something that's hoarded but something to be given freely. Money is a tool to make things better not just the means to build things bigger.

Encouragement flows through homes like electrical current. There are smiles everywhere and they make it almost impossible for frowns to linger for any length of time. Grief is met with comfort and joy with celebration. Quite a place, this place where generous people are. I'd like to live more of my life there, wouldn't you?

We can. In fact, the Bible says we are supposed to live there because it teaches that as stewards, we're responsible for living generously. I'm not just talking in relation to money here, although that's certainly important. But living generously means so much more than just money. Do we have a faith-building story to tell? Do we share it generously? Do we have a skill that is needed? Do we give it generously?

A man told me this story. He knew that God was speaking to him, but it was a hard message to accept.

The message was one word: Smile. No big deal, just smile. Except it was a big deal to the man and he argued that his mouth was too narrow and his front teeth were too crooked. As smiles went, his wasn't a very good one and, he felt, certainly wasn't something he thought he should be generous with. But God, as He usually does, was thinking differently and He shared this with the man. "I know your teeth are crooked but you do have many reasons to smile, and someone you'll meet today needs to see it. Your smile will be the only one they see all day and they won't care if it's not perfect; it will be enough. I want you to smile generously." As the man related his story to me, he shared that the words were almost a real conversation, and he still remembered it

Notes:

vividly. And you know what? When he started to be more generous with the imperfect smile that God gave him, and he quit worrying about his crooked teeth, and he started thinking about the person who needed to see his smile that day, he said something else happened. He found that he had more to smile about. As I listened to the story I thought of my own smile. Was I a good steward of it? Interesting to think about. The world could use more smiles—and it might actually be fun.

The fact is when we fulfill our responsibilities to be generous, our worlds—homes, schools, churches, workplaces, neighborhoods, wherever—are better places for us and those around us. Paul said this about generosity:

This most generous God who gives seed to the farmer that becomes bread for your meals is more than extravagant with you. He gives you something you can then give away, which grows into full-formed lives, robust in God, wealthy in every way, so that you can be generous in every way, producing with us great praise to God. Carrying out this social relief work involves far more than helping meet the bare needs of poor Christians. It also produces abundant and bountiful thanksgivings to God. (2 Corinthians 9:10-12, MSG)

The *New International Version* says it this way: "Now he who supplies seed to the sower and bread for food will also supply and increase your store of seed and will enlarge the harvest of your

---

Notes:

righteousness. You will be made rich in every way so that you can be generous on every occasion, and through us your generosity will result in thanksgiving to God."

There's a lot for us to think about here, so let's break the passage down into several thoughts.

- *We are in a position to be generous with others because God has been generous with us.* He's been, in fact, "extravagant" with us! Now, I understand that most of us aren't farmers, but God still provides us, figuratively, with seed. Remember chapter 7? God is the steward's source and He equips us with abilities that produce a good crop when we use them. It all begins with God.

- *When we are generous with what God has given to us, He increases His generosity to us.* Isn't that the meaning of the phrase "he will also ... increase your store of seed"? This is something we see again and again in Scripture and it's the subject for chapter 12, A Steward's Reward. Seeds are meant to be planted, but Scripture not only teaches that He will give us more seed, it connects the seeds we plant with two kinds of harvest. If this is true, then the steward who plants generously will actually produce more than she intended— and more than is possible with mere physical seeds. Here's the connection as recorded in the book of Isaiah: "As the rain and the snow come down from heaven, and do not return to it without watering the earth and making it bud and flourish, so that it yields seed for the sower and bread

Notes:

for the eater, so is my word that goes out from my mouth: it will not return to me empty, but will accomplish what I desire and achieve the purpose for which I sent it " (55:10-11). I think this means that the more generous we are with the gifts He's given *to* us, the more of His purpose He is able to accomplish *through* us.

- *The reason we are given more is so that we can give more.* In turn, does Paul say we'll have a tremendous harvest so we can fill more rented storage units? No, it's so that we'll have more to give away. And is Paul saying we "will be made rich in every way " so we'll have more? Hardly. The intention is for us to "be generous on every occasion." Is that something that appeals to you? Would you like to be part of that community that is defined by its generosity? Then *sow* more, *so* that you'll have more to *sow*. In other words, when we invest what God has given to us—whether time, talent, or treasure—His plan calls for our investment to increase, in order to put us in the position of being able to demonstrate even more generosity on future occasions.

- *Our generosity is an expression of worship and offering to God.* When we are people who act generously, others take note and "through us your generosity will result in thanksgiving to God." This is a great reminder that our generosity is only possible because He was generous to us first. When we keep that perspective, it's easier for us to step away from any temptation to take credit where credit is not due.

Notes:

If we took the time to think for a moment, we could probably recall many occasions when we would have liked to have been more generous but for one reason or another weren't able to. In Acts 3, Peter and John didn't have that much to give—or so it seemed: "Peter said, 'I don't have any money for you. But I'll give you what I have'" (verse 6, NLT). What Peter had was enough for a crippled man to get up and walk.

> **What Peter had was enough for a crippled man to get up and walk.**
> 🍂

We may not think we have much to give, but that would be wrong thinking. We can give whatever we do have, and give it generously. A smile? Who knows, it might come at just the right time. A note of encouragement? It might arrive when hope is nearly dead. A bag of groceries? Like the farmer's seed that brings a crop of righteousness, it might bring much more than a full stomach. After all, "It's not the one who plants or the one who waters who is at the center of this process but God, who makes things grow" (1 Corinthians 3:7, MSG).

A steward is responsible for living generously. Before we finish for the day, let's look at the question that was asked at the top of this chapter. When was the last time you met a truly generous grouch? I've asked that question hundreds of times and each time I've gotten the same response. First silence, as they replay a question that has two words that are not used together very often. Then a smile, as they realize it's a trick question. Finally recognition, as

Notes:

they come to the conclusion that grouches simply aren't known for their generosity. How would you answer this question? Have you ever met a truly generous person that you would also consider to be a grouch?

In chapter 14 we're going to look at The Paradox of Prosperity in a culture such as ours where the goal is to accumulate as much as possible. After all, our culture says accumulation is the path to happiness, and regards the truly generous person as something of a paradox. By one dictionary definition, a paradox is a statement contrary to received opinion. In our culture the "received opinion" advises us to find happiness, satisfaction, and contentment in the accumulation and abundance of things. Then shouldn't the wealthiest people be the most content and satisfied? Look around. Is the received opinion correct? Or do we find more than a fair share of discontent, anxiety, and despair in those whose primary goal is to acquire things?

Now let's look at those who are generous. The received opinion says that their sacrifices should bring a sense of lacking or emptiness, but that's not what we find. When I've asked the question about the truly generous grouch, it's been fascinating to watch the response. When people think about those they know who are generous, the one characteristic they all have in common is that they definitely are *not* grouches! On the contrary, the generous people we know are usually those who are most satisfied and content. I think generosity goes hand-in-hand with contentment and stinginess goes hand-in-hand with discontent. What does

Notes:

your experience confirm?

What an awesome thought, that we will "be made rich in every way so that [we] can be generous on every occasion." And an equally awesome thought is that the life of the generous person is characterized by the contentment and satisfaction that many of us seek. The promise of 2 Corinthians 9:10-11 is that our sowing reaps an unexpected harvest of contentment. If satisfaction and contentment are areas of contention in your life, maybe now is a good time to become more serious about your responsibilities as a steward. You won't regret it.

A Prayer for Your Day

Father, open my eyes and my heart to understand how generous You are with me. Help me to understand that Your generosity is my example, and that You have given me riches so that I can be a generous person myself. Move me deeper into a spirit of generosity and change my heart into one that gives—not just once in a while but on every occasion. It's not about what I can do but about what You have done. Keep this straight in my mind. Thank You that living generously is part of Your better way. Amen.

REFLECT & RESPOND

Have you ever met a truly generous grouch?

Describe how you feel when you are around a generous person.

What has God given you, money or otherwise, that you can share generously with others? How can you do a better job at doing this?

Paul says we are "made rich in every way so that [we] can be generous on every occasion." In which occasions is it most difficult for you to be generous? Ask God for His help to improve.

Would your closest acquaintances describe you more as a grouch or more as a generous person? Why?

CHAPTER ELEVEN

A Steward's Reality

Do we really believe our beliefs?

❦

Christ is the one through whom God created everything in
heaven and earth. He made the things we can see and the things
we can't see—kings, kingdoms, rulers, and authorities.
Everything has been created through him and for him.
—COLOSSIANS 1:16, NLT

In their excellent workbook for small group study titled *Experiencing God,* Henry Blackaby and Claude King make the following important observation: "What you do reveals what you believe about God, regardless of what you say."[1] Each of us needs to understand that the truth of this judgment is central to fulfilling our steward's responsibility and crucial to appropriating the steward's reality as it is described in the Scriptures.

The Oscar for Best Picture in 1981 was awarded to a very unlikely film. The story was primarily about the lives and athletic competitiveness of two men who ultimately earned gold medals in the 1924 Olympic Games held in Paris. The story was compelling and was presented well in the film, but it's the title that interests me right now. What was the origin of the expression

Chariots of Fire? I doubt whether very many of the film's viewers were aware that it was taken from an obscure and ancient event recorded in the Old Testament. I think the actual reference can help us understand how vast a steward's reality actually is, if we are truly willing to act on what we say we believe:

> So one night the king of Aram sent a great army with many chariots and horses to surround the city. When the servant of the man of God got up early the next morning and went outside, there were troops, horses, and chariots everywhere.
>
> "Ah, my lord, what will we do now?" he cried out to Elisha.
>
> "Don't be afraid!" Elisha told him. "For there are more on our side than on theirs!" Then Elisha prayed, "O LORD, open his eyes and let him see!" The LORD opened his servant's eyes, and when he looked up, he saw that the hillside around Elisha was filled with horses and chariots of fire. (2 Kings 6:14–17, NLT)

Please don't be turned off by unusual names and a story about something that happened thousands of years ago. There's something very valuable that each of us can learn here; the story points us to an exciting new dimension of a Steward's Journey. Elisha was an Old Testament prophet. The Bible says that he performed many miracles, spoke with God's authority, and, in the previous story, repeatedly thwarted the war plans of the king of Aram by giving advance warnings to Joram, Israel's king. Like modern politicians, the king of Aram was concerned about leaks from within his closest circle of

Notes:

advisors, and he tried to identify a traitor among them. Eventually, however, he discovered that Elisha was the source of his problem. Acting again like a modern leader, the king tried to eliminate the problem by sending his soldiers to capture Elisha. Aram's army was the unwelcome sight that greeted Elisha's servant one morning as he discovered that he and his master were outnumbered. Surrounded, Elisha's servant wondered what they would do next.

Isn't it interesting, though, that the reality seen by Elisha was not the same reality seen by his servant? Through a lifetime of obedience Elisha had learned he could trust God for resources that weren't readily apparent to others—that were beyond the everyday reality of most people. *But they were there, nonetheless!* Look closely at how Elisha responded to his servant or, more to the point, look at how he didn't respond. Elisha didn't ask God to send help. Why? Because the reality of the situation was that God's help was already present! Instead, Elisha asked God to reveal to the servant the help that was already there. He asked God to

> **It is in our actions that we reveal the personal realities we define for ourselves.**
> ❦

let the servant view the true reality of the circumstance. Here were two men, both Elisha and his servant, apparently surrounded by overwhelming obstacles, yet until Elisha's prayer was answered, only one of them understood the true reality of the situation.

A steward's reality is similar. It often involves resources that are beyond the scope of our natural eyes, minds, and imaginations.

Notes:

Stewards who have learned to depend on God have *experienced God.* They've gained an ability to see beyond what their senses tell them and discover provisions that are beyond the natural realm. These provisions reflect the reality that is always present to the steward in the realm of the *super*natural. Let's take this a step further by looking at several Bible references that describe resources that cannot be measured with a purely natural mind-set.

The Colossians 1:16 reference at the top of this chapter is only one of many addressing this subject. Here are some more:

> The earth is the LORD's, and everything in it, the world, and all who live in it. (Psalm 24:1)

> "The earth," after all, "is God's, and everything in it." (1 Corinthians 10:26, MSG)

> Yes! Everything in heaven, everything on earth; the kingdom all yours! You've raised yourself high over all. Riches and glory come from you, you're ruler over all; You hold strength and power in the palm of your hand to build up and strengthen all. (1 Chronicles 29:11-12, MSG)

> "The silver is mine and the gold is mine," declares the LORD Almighty. (Haggai 2:8)

> Everything under heaven belongs to me. (Job 41:11)

Notes:

"For all the animals of the forest are mine, and I own the cattle on a thousand hills. Every bird of the mountains and all the animals of the field belong to me. If I were hungry, I would not mention it to you, for all the world is mine and everything in it." (Psalm 50:10-12, NLT)

You can be sure that God will take care of everything you need. (Philippians 4:19, MSG)

Unfortunately, however, these references are reduced to mere words unless our *actions* declare them to be true. It isn't enough for us to profess belief in something by routinely singing hymns or regularly reciting the historical creeds of the church. No, as Blackaby and King pointed out, it is in our *actions* that we reveal the personal realities we define for ourselves. The sad thing about this is that our realities are *always* smaller than what God intends for us. What a shame.

A glance at a local newspaper will reveal examples of how tragic it is to live in a reduced reality. Occasionally, articles will feature a story describing the life of a person who died in absolutely poverty-stricken surroundings. Often neighbors who are interviewed describe a lonely existence and one that gave absolutely no clues to what was found after the person's death. The indigent person died rich. Very rich. Sometimes there are even cash caches discovered throughout the apartment. Or perhaps the authorities found paper trails leading them to a previously unknown bank

Notes:

account or a safe-deposit box containing great wealth. These stories aren't common but they appear often enough that they cause me to ask *why?* Why would a person of such wealth exist in such poverty? What would make a person hoard money so jealously that any usefulness it might have had was completely lost to them? *Why?* It doesn't make sense.

My fear is that too many people of faith, people who profess belief in a God with unlimited resources at His disposal, voluntarily limit themselves to a reality that is much smaller than what He intends for them. Their professions of trust in God's provisions are cancelled out by lives that deny Him the opportunity to work on their behalf. Like the impoverished wealthy person in the newspaper, they will never know what they have missed.

Rev. E. M. Clark is a longtime minister who chronicled many of his faith-building stewardship experiences in his self-published book, *How to Be Happy Giving Your Money Away.*[2] In a ministry that spanned more than half a century, Rev. Clark has given away far more money than is possible to explain in a purely natural realm, but his reality was far greater than what natural eyes can see. In the process, Rev. Clark confirmed with his actions that He believed God would make resources available to faithful stewards. Imagine the thrills he and his wife experienced, thrills that came from continually trusting God for the impossible and then watching it become reality. I've known a tiny fraction of that in my own life and there's nothing like it.

A Steward's Journey positions us to share a new reality, but

Notes:

only when we believe our beliefs. Has everything really been created through Him and for Him? Our actions reveal our answer. Does the earth, everything in it, and all who live in it truly belong to Him? If we believe it we need to live it. On a more personal level, is it possible that God really can and will take care of everything we need? Or, like the example of the wealthy person who died in poverty, do we consign ourselves to a reduced reality that never fully benefits from a steward's experience of God?

A Steward's Journey is not about having less because we have given, it is about experiencing more because we have lived the reality promised to those who are faithful. A Steward's Journey is about living life to its fullest. I urge you to stay on the journey.

A Prayer for Your Day

Heavenly Father, open our eyes and let us see the true reality of our circumstances and the provision that You want to bring to faithful stewards. Help us to experience this reality and give us the courage to act on our beliefs. Teach us in ways we can't imagine. Surprise us with Your faithfulness. Make us into people of faith who act upon what we profess. Keep us from empty professions of faith and bring us into full expressions of our trust in You. Amen.

❧

REFLECT & RESPOND

Scripture says that we can be "sure that God will take care of everything you need" (Philippians 4:19, MSG). Reflect on whether your *actions* confirm or deny the reality of this promise.

If there are areas in your life that overwhelm and defeat you, consider praying Elisha's prayer: "Father, open my eyes to see Your reality in this circumstance."

List three or four areas of your life where you would like to close the gap between your beliefs and your actions, then identify one specific thing that you can *do* to act more consistently with your beliefs. Ask God to help you accomplish this successfully.

Read *How to Be Happy Giving Your Money Away* or another faith-building book, such as *The Autobiography of George Muller*,[3] to see examples of what can happen when actions conform to beliefs.

Chapter Twelve

A Steward's Reward

Here's the secret to discovering
God's will for your life.

❧

The master said, "Well done, my good and faithful
servant. You have been faithful in handling this
small amount, so now I will give you many
more responsibilities. Let's celebrate together!"
—Matthew 25:23, nlt

I'd like you to consider something with me. Imagine a birthday cake with five small candles and the playful energy and noise of kids playing games at the party. Picture the eagerness when the birthday boy rips the wrapping off his presents. Then he comes to one last gift from me, his father, but it's too huge and he needs help unwrapping it. Now imagine what you would think if the gift was a stack of lumber, a powerful top-of-the-line Sears Crafts-man twelve-inch table saw, and a note saying "Have fun!" What kind of father would you think I was? Loving? Responsible? No! You'd think I was kidding. Compare that with a different birth-day scene. In this one I give my son a small, safe woodworking tool and over the next weeks and months I patiently spend the time to teach him how to use it properly. Which gift would be in the best interest of a five-year-old? It's easy to see, isn't it?

I wish that we could see our relationship with God as clearly, and understand the parallels between how He works in our lives and how we act in the lives of our chil-

> **A steward's rewards follow a steward's faithfulness. That's a principle of stewardship.**
> 🍂

dren. As parents we should understand that it can be inherently dangerous for us to reward our children with too much too soon. Instead, we wait until our children earn our trust and can handle what they already have before we reward them with more. God does

the same with us. A steward's rewards follow a steward's faithfulness. That's a principle of stewardship. When we master the smaller things we are rewarded with larger ones. It's that simple. Often though, we act as if God will ignore this principle and reward us before it would be wise to do so.

I know that on more than one occasion I've been guilty of asking God for some powerful top-of-the-line answers to prayer when I haven't quite mastered some of the simpler answers He's already given me. Have you? Why is it that we expect God to give us direction in the big things of our lives when we're not obediently following His direction in the smaller things? As a father, if I saw that my son hadn't quite grasped all that he needed to know about the basics of carpentry, how wrong, unwise, and potentially dangerous would it be for me to prematurely push him into a level

Notes:

that is beyond his demonstrated abilities? Yet we often act as if we expect God to move us into challenges, opportunities, and blessings that are beyond the obedience and faithfulness that we've already demonstrated.

Virtually everyone I know that professes faith in God says they'd like to know what His will for their life is. Who wouldn't? When I have given talks about the subject in the past I've usually included this question: "How many would like to know what God's will is for your lives?" I'd follow up with a seemingly preposterous and presumptuous statement: *I can tell you what God's will for your life is.* You can imagine the response, *"Excuse me? You can tell people what God's will is for them?"* Yes, actually, and based on the principle outlined in Matthew 25 so could you. So here it is, the secret to discovering God's will for our lives: *God wants us to do what He's already told us to do, but we haven't done yet.* Very simple, isn't it? But it's hardly a secret, it's a basic stewardship principle that forms the foundation of a steward's reward: *faithfulness over little leads to responsibility over more.* If we want to know what God has for us in the future, then we need to do what He's told us to do in the past.

The reference in Matthew 25 talks extensively about the steward's reward. Sometimes that reward is the positive one given in the beginning of this chapter: "Well done, my good and faithful servant. You have been faithful in handling this small amount, so now I will give you many more responsibilities." Unfortunately, the reward, or we might say the consequence of the steward's

Notes:

action, is not always a positive one. When we continue to read the passage we discover that one of the servants didn't act faithfully. He was afraid, so he dug a hole to hide and protect what had been given to him. He didn't follow the example he'd seen his master demonstrate many times before; he didn't invest what he had been given. This servant acted out of his fear, and he also received a "reward." Here's what he was told: "Well, you should at least have put my money into the bank so I could have some interest. Take the money from this servant and give it to the one with the ten bags of gold. To those who use well what they are given, even more will be given, and they will have an abundance. But from those who are unfaithful, even what little they have will be taken away" (Matthew 25:27-29, NLT).

We may not like the concept of negative rewards but it's a concept that Jesus clearly taught. As parents we often employ the same principle with our children. How would we respond if we were notified that our teenage son was stopped by the police for driving recklessly? Would we rush out to buy him a new and more powerful car? Or would we take his keys away and watch him more carefully in the future until he began acting with more maturity? I think we can agree there's only one responsible choice, and yet there are times when we wonder why God doesn't reward our irresponsible behavior. On a Steward's Journey we need to remember that God has two options in response to the quality of our stewardship, and that He will always select the one that reinforces more mature and responsible behaviors in us.

Notes:

We don't always see the extent of our reward immediately and my mind is drawn to two examples in the New Testament to illustrate this. The first describes a young boy with very little; in fact, all he had to share were two fish and five small loaves of bread. This is how John records what happened:

> Then Andrew, Simon Peter's brother, spoke up. "There's a young boy here with five barley loaves and two fish. But what good is that with this huge crowd?"
>
> "Tell everyone to sit down," Jesus ordered. So all of them—the men alone numbered five thousand—sat down on the grassy slopes. Then Jesus took the loaves, gave thanks to God, and passed them out to the people. Afterward he did the same with the fish. And they all ate until they were full. "Now gather the leftovers," Jesus told his disciples, "so that nothing is wasted." There were only five barley loaves to start with, but twelve baskets were filled with the pieces of the bread the people did not eat! (John 6:8-13, NLT)

Imagine the excitement later that night when the small boy told his parents what happened to him that day! That would have been a show-and-tell for the ages, and right at center stage was a little boy who was willing to give up what little he had.

Contrast the boy's experience with the rich ruler who questioned Jesus about how he could live forever. *The Message* describes their exchange this way:

Notes:

"If you want to give it all you've got," Jesus replied, "go sell your possessions; give everything to the poor. All your wealth will then be in heaven. Then come follow me." That was the last thing the young man expected to hear. And so, crestfallen, he walked away. He was holding on tight to a lot of things, and he couldn't bear to let go. (Matthew 19:21-22)

The *New International Version* says that the young man "went away sad." Now imagine the scene in the home of the rich young ruler. He had gone to ask Jesus how he could have eternal life and came away with the realization that his possessions would keep him from attaining it. No wonder he went away sad.

I think about these two stories often and in my own imagination I wonder what life would have been like for them when they were much older. Perhaps they were grandfathers. Both would be witnesses to the social, cultural, and spiritual revolution resulting from the dynamic transformation of the disciples after Jesus' crucifixion and resurrection. The world was changing literally before their eyes. I imagine the ruler, still with his riches, looking in from the outside. He had much, he had a chance to be part of history, but the price was too high. His memories were of what might have been. Then my mind pictures another house. A little boy runs excitedly to his grandfather and begs, "Papa, Papa, tell me again

> **Faithfulness over a little leads to responsibility over more.**
> ❧

Notes:

about the time you gave your lunch to Jesus and he fed thou-sands…" He only had a little, but he gave what he had. And do you know what? My imagination isn't big enough to capture how good he must have felt.

There's one more passage we need to review before we finish discussing a steward's reward. *Please,* pay attention to these words in Luke 16:10-11. They are crucial if you ever want to acquire *true riches*: "Whoever can be trusted with very little can also be trusted with much, and whoever is dishonest with very little will also be dishonest with much. So if you have not been trustworthy in handling worldly wealth, who will trust you with true riches?" Now consider these four things about this verse:

1. It indicates that the way we deal with small responsibilities is the way we will deal with large responsibilities. We can-not pretend that we will be more responsible and more generous when we have more; the pattern we establish with little is the pattern of our life. This is a consistent connection throughout the scripture.

2. It makes a point of saying that the opposite of being trust-worthy is being dishonest. The dictionary defines dishonest as being disposed to lie, cheat, defraud, or deceive. Ouch! That's an unusually frank and negative description of who we are when we don't live up to our responsibilities as stewards, and it may not be a description that we initially accept. Think about it, though, and see whether or not it is true in your life.

Notes:

3. It distinguishes between the two concepts of worldly wealth and true riches. Worldly wealth we understand as things like money, possessions, and power, but what are true riches? Could they be those things that money can't buy? Things like contentment and joy in your family—or a healing touch, divine presence, or teaching with authority in your church?

4. Even though it distinguishes between worldly wealth and true riches, the verse clearly links the two. Proving ourselves trustworthy in the handling of our money and possessions is absolutely essential to receiving true riches. If this verse followed the design of a college catalog it would say that we have to prove ourselves in the course of worldly wealth as a prerequisite for enrolling in the course on true riches. Yet too many of us seem to be looking for a graduate education in true riches before we've successfully passed the undergraduate course in worldly wealth. The verse in Luke says that simply won't work.

Matthew 25:23 concludes with these words: "Let's celebrate together!" (NLT). Talk about a reward! That's about as good as it gets in the eternal scheme of things. My prayer for each of us today is that we will all live in such a way that eventually we will hear and experience the reward of a good steward. "Well done! You have been faithful! Let's celebrate together!"

Notes:

A Prayer for Your Day

Heavenly Father, teach us the connection between
worldly wealth and true riches in our own lives. Give us
a glimpse of what it will mean for us to hear You say
"well done" by making true riches the most important
part of our lives. Pour Your riches through us and into
the lives of those who need Your presence. Amen.

❧

Reflect & Respond

If we want to know what God has for us in the future then we need to do what He's told us to do in the past. Reflect on whether you have "unfinished business" in the past that is hindering your opportunities in the future.

Consider whether your handling of worldly wealth is closer to the experience of the young boy with the loaves and fishes (reward) or that of the rich young ruler (regret).

We cannot pretend that we will be more responsible and more generous when we have more; the pattern we establish with little is the pattern of our life. How do your life experiences and actions confirm or refute this sentence?

Living More With Less

CHAPTER THIRTEEN

Follow the Money

Money is a spiritual barometer of
our heart's openness to God.

❧

*Wherever your treasure is, there your
heart and thoughts will also be.*

—MATTHEW 6:21, NLT

God doesn't need our money! This point needs to be crystal clear as the road of *A Steward's Journey* turns to the subject of giving in the following chapters. Without this understanding, we are very likely to misinterpret the value of giving, carry a distorted view of stewardship through life, and miss the fulfillment that only a giver knows. God desires more for us and that's the reason I want to start this section with a look at the biblical link between our money and our heart.

Whether you've been part of the church for a long or short time, or even if you're not part of the church, you've probably heard the charge that all the church is concerned about is money. Is the accusation fair? Think for a moment about the difficulty facing a pastor when he approaches this subject. With nearly 2,300 references in the Bible on the general topic of money and possessions, a pastor has plenty of sermon material. Yet for a variety of reasons many pastors limit their discussion of stewardship to just a few weeks each year. But pity the poor pastor who preaches one sermon on the topic of money a year and it just happens to be the same Sunday that infrequent attenders appear in the pew. Other than Christmas or Easter it might be the only week they show up, but from their limited experience and perspective the pastor "only talks about money." So what's true here? Is it all about the money, or is money just a spiritual barometer of our heart's openness to God?

In the reference at the beginning of this chapter, Jesus links our treasure with our hearts. Let me illustrate that link with a modern example. Suppose you learn from a very knowledgeable friend that the stock of a company you've never heard about before is well positioned to increase dramatically in the near future. As a result of what you hear you decide to buy some shares of the company's common stock. An interesting thing happens next. Your behavior changes, and if you're like most people, the chances are

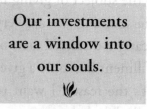

Our investments are a window into our souls.

very good that you'll begin doing something you've never done before. Maybe you'll use the newspaper or maybe you'll look on the Internet, but you'll start following the company's stock performance regularly. The reason for this sudden interest is the link between our treasure and our heart. When we invest our treasure in something, our heart inevitably

---

Notes:

follows. We become involved in our investment. We want to know how it's performing. Our behavior proves that the way we spend our money changes the way we live our lives. Think about it. Our behavior proves that our investments have consequences that directly affect how we live. It's true. Our investments are a window into our souls.

Jesus knew this in His encounter with the rich young ruler described by Matthew. The young man had mastered all of the external requirements his religious heritage had taught him, but there was something missing. Jesus looked into his soul and saw a void; the young man's love of God was not equal to his love of wealth:

> "I've obeyed all these commandments," the young man
> replied. "What else must I do?" Jesus told him, "If you want
> to be perfect, go and sell all you have and give the money to
> the poor, and you will have treasure in heaven. Then come,
> follow me." But when the young man heard this, he went
> sadly away because he had many possessions. (Matthew
> 19:20-22, NLT)

Jesus knew that if the young man had been willing to invest his treasure in heaven that his life-commitment would also be focused on heaven-centered activities. The issue was about money, at least externally, because Jesus understood that it formed a barrier to pleasing God and that the young man was unwilling to take the

---

Notes:

barrier down. For the rich young ruler, was it a matter of the money or of the heart? The fact is that his money *revealed* his heart.

We've all heard, though, that every rule has exceptions and the Scriptures have stories of how money has been used to try to bribe God rather than please Him. I think these examples help show us that God's priority is really about the condition of our hearts and not the size of our gifts. Otherwise, if God was primarily interested in our money, He would never reject offerings the way He did in the Old Testament. God is not willing to accept gifts from us when they are given as a bribe to continue living a lifestyle that displeases Him. Here are two stories that illustrate this point.

Isaiah was an Old Testament prophet who was one of God's primary spokesmen to ancient Israel. Here's how he expressed God's feelings about those who thought their money would be enough to buy themselves into God's good graces: "'The multitude of your sacrifices—what are they to me?' says the LORD" (Isaiah 1:11). Isaiah goes on to say this in verse 13: "Stop bringing meaningless offerings! Your incense is detestable to me." The *New Living Translation* words it like this: "I am sick of your sacrifices. The incense you bring me is a stench in my nostrils" (verses 11,13). Ouch! This outright rejection of Israel's offerings doesn't sound to me like the action of a God who is only concerned about money. Instead, it sounds to me like God is primarily interested in the type of people we are, our motives, and the

Notes:

way we live our lives. When our motives and lives align with His purposes, then and only then are our offerings acceptable to Him. But when we live our lives in opposition to what He desires for us, it is not possible for us to cover our rebellion with false offerings.

Several generations earlier, Israel's last judge, Samuel, shared the same message with Saul, Israel's first king. Even though he had been directed to destroy all of the livestock when he conquered the people known as Amalekites, Saul thought he knew better and kept the best animals to offer as a sacrifice to God. It was a big mistake. Rather than welcoming the offering, God rejected it. Samuel explained the reason to Saul: "Do you think all GOD wants are sacrifices—empty rituals just for show? He wants you to listen to him! Plain listening is the thing, not staging a lavish religious production" (1 Samuel 15:22, MSG). Another version translates the verse this way: "What is more pleasing to the LORD: your burnt offerings and sacrifices or your obedience to his voice? Obedience is far better than sacrifice" (NLT).

Saul's offering was rejected because it was offered in disobedience. The ancient Israelites were told not to even bother with their offerings because their disobedience had become offensive to God. That doesn't sound to me like God's focus is on money. His interest in our openness to His purpose in our lives far exceeds any monetary gift we could give Him.

Writing in his letter to the church in Corinth, Paul says, "You must each make up your own mind as to how much you should

---

Notes:

give. Don't give reluctantly or in response to pressure. For God loves the person who gives cheerfully" (2 Corinthians 9:7, NLT). John's first letter also clarifies how God regards our offerings. While written in the context of our receiving from God rather than giving to Him, I think it makes an important distinction between the things that we do and the reasons behind why we do them: "Dear friends, if our hearts do not condemn us, we have confidence before God and receive from him anything we ask, because we obey his commands and do what pleases him" (1 John 3:21-22).

I absolutely love the way John makes a distinction between our *mere obedience* to God's commands and our *pleasing* God. I've known people who have rigidly tried to follow commandments by strictly adhering to a set of legal rules, but I'm not at all certain that God is pleased with that. In fact, I think the lesson of the Bible clearly shows that He is not. The Israelites were following the narrow letter of the law when they brought their offerings, but they certainly displeased God in the process. What I'm suggesting to you is that if we bring our offerings to God reluctantly, or in response to pressure, or because we are trying to fulfill a religious obligation, God takes no pleasure in our gifts. His desire is that we give cheerfully because cheerful giving is a reflection of a grateful heart. And the offering of our heart is what really matters to God.

Is it all about the money? Or is it about something more? What does your heart tell you?

Notes:

A Prayer for Your Day

*Heavenly Father, renew in me a heart that wants to
please You. Accept my offerings because they are genuinely given from a steward's heart. Guard my heart by
guiding my investments into those things that matter.
Amen.*

REFLECT & RESPOND

When God looks at your investments, what conclusion does He make about the openness of your heart to Him?

"God loves it when the giver delights in the giving" (2 Corinthians 9:7, MSG). Describe how you think God responds to your gifts.

On a scale of 1 (opportunity) to 10 (obligation), how would you describe your giving? Consider things you could do to make your giving less of an obligation and ask for God's help in making this so.

Is your legacy closer to the joy and memories of the small boy who gave the loaves and fish, or the material wealth of the ruler who held onto what he had? Why?

CHAPTER FOURTEEN

The Paradox
of Prosperity

Generosity, not accumulation, is the path to prosperity.

❧

*A stingy man is eager to get rich and is
unaware that poverty awaits him.*

—PROVERBS 28:22

A generous man will himself be blessed.

—PROVERBS 22:9

In an earlier chapter we talked about the word *generosity* and how
it was a word that felt good. Today we're going to talk about
stingy. If generosity is a soft down comforter on a cold winter
night, stingy is a scratchy wool shirt on a hot summer day. One is
warm and inviting, the other harsh and unappealing.

Stingy just doesn't feel good. Not only that, but the most powerful observation from Proverbs 28:22 about being stingy is that
it doesn't work! It doesn't get us where we want to go! In fact, it
leads to an unintended consequence that is exactly opposite of
what we desire. I'm afraid, though, that many of us might doubt

whether this Proverb is true. We have, after all, seen apparent evidence to the contrary—in lives that seem to personify stinginess with none of the downside the Proverb describes. That's why this chapter is titled the Paradox of Prosperity, because sometimes things aren't what they seem to be. Earlier we defined *paradox* as "a statement contrary to received opinion." Another definition says that it is a "seemingly contradictory statement that may nonetheless be true." The essence of a paradox can create difficulties for us when we try to understand the truth of the Proverb because being stingy can seem to work, at least on the surface. These appearances can raise doubts about whether the Proverb actually reflects reality. What's true here? Does stingy work for us or against us?

I think the world of our own experiences has some clues to help us determine the answer to these questions. All other things being equal, who would we rather be around, a stingy person or a generous one? Let's say we had two acquaintances that suddenly needed our help: one well known for hoarding what they had and living a self-centered existence, the other who enjoyed a reputation as a giver, constantly reaching out to and doing things for others. Which would we rather help and, if we could only assist one, who would it be?

Or, for those of us who are married, think about this: What if you awoke one day and thought to yourself, *I'm only capable of a certain amount of love, so I'm going to hold on to what I have. I'd better not give any away or do anything that would reduce what I*

Notes:

have. I need it all. Are alarm bells going off? It's not even pleasant to think about the consequences of acting that way in a marriage, is it? Why? Because experience tells us that giving love leads to receiving more love in return, whereas selfishly holding on is the certain path to having less. Or, put another way, the stingy spouse will come to ruin but the generous spouse will be refreshed.

There are examples of this principle in operation all around us. Several years ago my wife Pam and I were fortunate enough to visit Israel. Early one morning our group traveled to the northern border of the country, to a vibrant oasis with cold flowing water and lush green vegetation. It was a nature reserve not too far from the headwaters of the Dan River. Eventually the Dan would join other streams, become the River Jordan, and flow a short distance into the Sea of Galilee. The Galilee is a large lake that the ancient historian Josephus described as a region renowned for the fertility of its soil. We saw the shores of the Galilee, still productive and full of life.

The Jordan empties from the southern edge of the Galilee and forms the tenuous West Bank between Israel and Jordan. It flows southward with crops and vegetation lining its banks.

We drove the road that paralleled the Jordan, where it fed into a second large lake, but there was a noticeable difference in this body of water. There was none of the life that we saw surrounding the Galilee. What a contrast those two lakes were, one surrounded by life and the other by virtually nothing. Why? The same water source fed both. What was the difference? The Sea of Galilee teems

Notes:

with life because it not only accepts water from rivers flowing into it but it also releases water into rivers flowing out. The Dead Sea is stagnant because it only accepts water but releases none; the Dead Sea has no outlet. The Jordan flows *through* the Galilee but it *stops* in the Dead Sea. One lake gives and lives, the other holds on to what it has, and its description became its name.

People can be like that, and so can churches and organizations. When I think about organizations like the Salvation Army, the word *generous* comes to mind. But I've also experienced other organizations, many of which no longer prosper or exist, that were defined by selfishness. Like the examples of well-known but fraudulently operated corporations like Enron, they took care of themselves at the expense of others, a path that eventually led to their ruin.

My guess is that each of us could identify examples of generous and selfish people or organizations from our experiences. Sometimes the ultimate consequences of their stingy actions may not be readily apparent. Sometimes, the truth of the proverb takes time to unfold. Sometimes, its truth is hidden from our view behind a facade of empty possessions. The truth is that more than one stingy person has had to move from their luxurious, comfortable homes into sparse, cramped quarters including, in some cases, prison. Ultimately the stingy will come to ruin and the generous to prosperity, even if the unique circumstances for each may be hard for us to fathom and require us to exercise more than a little amount of faith.

Notes:

One dictionary definition of stingy says "selfishly unwilling to share with others." I seriously doubt whether anyone reading *A Steward's Journey* would like to be called selfish or be known for their unwillingness to share. In fact, I suspect those descriptions run counter to some of our earliest memories. How many of us were taught almost from the time we can remember, that we were supposed to share? I'd also be surprised if many of us didn't have *don't be selfish* messages ringing in our ears long before we walked through the door on our first day of kindergarten. Right? Then don't you think that it's highly unlikely we would often think of ourselves as stingy, or want others to think so, *even if it's true?*

There's an important reason for us to spend time on this, and it has to do with a single word in the Proverb: *unaware*. By definition, we're not going to be prepared for something that catches us unaware. That's the reason I'm asking each of us to consider and closely examine our stewardship of money, and whether we tend toward stinginess or generosity. Because it's not good to be caught unaware, to strive for one thing only to end up with a far different and disastrous result. It can happen, though, if we're not careful, and this Proverb focuses our attention on an area that can have potentially devastating consequences if we miss our target.

One of the reasons we are unaware is that we don't think of ourselves as stingy. Instead, we would probably choose other descriptions that are more flattering. We might describe ourselves as being *prudent,* or consider ourselves wise for taking the *conservative* course. There's nothing wrong with exercising *caution,* after

---

Notes:

all, and it's certainly good to be *frugal* in the event that some calamity comes our way in the future. Most of us can fill in the blank with a list of comfortable adjectives we would use to describe ourselves and these certainly may be accurate descriptions. The challenge is knowing whether we are being truthful with ourselves or are trying to avoid dealing with our own stinginess.

Please don't misunderstand. Just because people are prudent, cautious, conservative, or frugal doesn't mean they're stingy. *But it doesn't mean they aren't either.* What's the difference? Proverbs 28:22 points us to the heart of the matter which, like many other things in life, turns out to be a matter of the heart. Using both Proverbs and dictionary definitions, let's examine some characteristics of those who are stingy. They are traits we can all use to double-check our own attitude toward generosity and stinginess.

The stingy person is *selfish*. "Forget about anyone else, it's all about me." We've all known people like this and too often no matter how hard we might try we can't forget them. It's too bad, isn't it, that there are some people from our past that we'd just as soon forget? Why? Because it was all about them.

The stingy person is *unwilling to share*. "I don't want to, I don't have to, and I'm not going to." People like this could share, they just don't. The unsharing person can often leave an almost tragically uncaring wake wherever they've been. Many times they are people of considerable resources that could have filled many unmet needs if they'd only been shared.

The stingy person is *unsuspecting*. "What poverty? I'm doing

---

Notes:

just fine, I've got everything I need." People who are alert and aware, as opposed to unsuspecting, would never start across a bridge if they knew floodwaters had just washed away its center span. To them, the bridge is the way to get to their destination. But intentions are not enough to arrive at the destination if danger signs along the way are ignored.

I grew up involved in sports and there's a great basketball illustration that I hope can help us understand this principle. Some players seem to bring out the best in their teammates. They thrive on it. They understand the concept that success involves more than what can be accomplished as individuals. You find these players passing up good shots to feed assists to others who have better ones. Defensively, they know when to pick up the slack if their teammates are in trouble. Do you know what these players are called? Winners.

There's another group of players, unfortunately a much larger one. They hog the ball on offense and play soft defense so they can have fresh legs on the end of the court where statistics matter. The game isn't spelled T-E-A-M, it's spelled T-H-E-M. It's all about them. Very rarely, though, do these players wear championship rings. Their stinginess makes it almost impossible to achieve the ultimate victory, and they usually bounce from team to team soon after wearing out their welcome. Let's learn from their example.

> **The seeds of stinginess will not produce a crop of generosity.**
> 🌱

Notes:

I hope that you've started to think about the Paradox of Prosperity because understanding the paradox is crucial to releasing the benefits of generosity in your life. Once again, let's look at Solomon's words from the book of Ecclesiastes, this time from *The Message*:

> Everything I wanted I took—I never said no to myself. I gave
> in to every impulse, held back nothing. I sucked the marrow
> of pleasure out of every task—my reward to myself for a hard
> day's work! Then I took a good look at everything I'd done,
> looked at all the sweat and hard work. But when I looked, I
> saw nothing but smoke. Smoke and spitting into the wind.
> There was nothing to any of it. Nothing. (2:10-11)

Holding on to what we have is not the way to prosperity. Generosity is.

The best way to have a friend is to be a friend. The best way to be loved is to love. The best way to be blessed is to bless. The best way to experience generosity is to be generous. Understanding the Paradox of Prosperity can be as easy as recognizing this simple truth: we will all reap what we sow. The seeds of stinginess will not produce a crop of generosity. Understanding the Paradox of Prosperity can be a transforming moment in our lives. In another proverb, Solomon wrote this: "Wisdom is supreme; therefore get wisdom. Though it cost all you have, get understanding. Esteem her, and she will exalt you; embrace her, and she will honor you"

Notes:

(Proverbs 4:7-8). Wouldn't it be great, and wouldn't our world be a better place, if the full wisdom and understanding of the Paradox of Prosperity became a part of who we are?

A Prayer for Your Day

Heavenly Father, create in us a new spirit of generosity and keep us from being deceived by the constant voices that tell us the way to prosperity is to hold on to what we have. Help us to discover the thrill of sharing that only a faithful steward can know. Use us to do Your work and to make the lives of those around us better because we are faithful to Your calling. Amen.

🌿

REFLECT & RESPOND

On a generosity scale of 1 (soft down comforter) to 10 (scratchy wool shirt), how would you describe yourself?

Using the same scale, how do you think your friends would answer this question about you?

Describe your feelings when you are in the prolonged presence of a stingy person. A generous person.

What two or three specific things can you change this week to help you become a more generous person?

CHAPTER FIFTEEN

Excellent Giving

Excellence is not accidental. Excellence is intentional.

❦

But just as you excel in everything—in faith,
in speech, in knowledge, in complete
earnestness and in your love for us—see that you
also excel in this grace of giving.

—2 CORINTHIANS 8:7

When most of us think of the Olympic Games, several images probably come to mind. Perhaps they are memories of elaborate Opening Ceremonies in past Olympic Games that we've seen on television, the grace and beauty of the figure skaters, the strength and endurance of the track and field athletes, the remarkable balance and skill of the gymnast, or the national anthem of the gold medalist's country as the winning athlete stands on the top step of the awards platform. My guess is that all of the Olympic moments share at least one thing in common: they occurred in front of large crowds and were televised to hundreds of millions more worldwide. In these moments we watch the world's best athletes perform at the peak of their abilities and at the height of their athletic careers. Yet few of us may ever stop to consider what it took to reach this pinnacle—the unpublicized personal sacrifices that paved the way for Olympic success.

I doubt that many of us can imagine how many falls and bruises it took for the figure skaters or the gymnasts to perfect their routines. I'm not sure anyone but the distance runner can truly appreciate the amount of emotionally isolating and physically exhausting miles that must be traveled to properly train for an Olympic marathon. As we watch the sprinters strain to hit the finish line first, we don't think about the depths of diets, deprivation, and discipline it took for them to get there. When we cheer the winning goal in ice hockey we're largely unaware of the sacrifices made by parents to get their sons to predawn practice because it's the only time available at the ice rink.

The Olympic Games are more than spotlights, precision choreography, and brightly colored costumes. They are weeks, months, and years of practice; uncounted aching, strained, and torn muscles; and unseen psychological battles that lead some to a champion's confidence and others to abandon the effort.

Olympic athletes understand that excellence is not accidental. They dedicate themselves so thoroughly to their strict practice routines because they know that excellence is the product of being intentional. You might not see the similarity at first, but I think there's a principle at work here that is similar to the reference from Corinthians at the beginning of this chapter: "Excel in this grace of giving," Paul said. His words show that he didn't believe giving was something that could be approached casually. He challenged

Notes:

his readers to make the same commitment to excellence in their giving as they made in other areas of their lives.

Paul's challenge is just as valid for us today as it was when it was written. The question, though, is how? How do we achieve excellence in giving or, asking an even broader question, how do we achieve excellence in anything? The key to getting better at anything we do is to practice.

Practice prepares us for excellence, whether in giving, athletics, or any other aspect of our lives. At least it does if we approach practice properly and understand the characteristics of practice that make it so valuable. I'd like us to review some of these characteristics now.

PRACTICE HAS A PURPOSE

It's not enough for an athlete to spend hours each day on the football field or baseball diamond. There needs to be organization to the practice that leads to accomplishing a specific goal. Journalists who want to win the Pulitzer Prize will dedicate themselves to improving their writing and reporting skills more than those who just want to earn a paycheck. As we read in chapter 10, Paul says that our goal of excellence in giving should take us to the point where we can be generous on every occasion. Each of us should look at how we are practicing excellence in giving, and whether our practice regimen will result in the generosity Paul describes.

Notes:

Practice Involves Repetition

How many times do executive chefs prepare their gourmet meals until they are satisfied that the meal will come out exactly right, *every time?* The answer: countless. Why? Because repetition increases our skill at performing a task. Sure, it's possible for someone to have beginners luck *once,* but to find those who consistently deliver high quality, all we have to do is look for those who have practiced their skill repeatedly until they achieved a level of excellence. In the next chapter we'll talk more about the importance of a systematic and repetitive approach to giving.

Practice Becomes a Lifestyle

If we want to achieve *and maintain* excellence in anything we do, it has to become a regular part of our lives. I have a friend who is an excellent violinist and I don't think there's a day in his life when he doesn't practice. Playing the violin, and playing it well, has become part of his lifestyle.

There was a time not too many years ago when professional athletes took time off from their conditioning regimens during the off-season. Not any longer. The levels of excellence in professional athletics today demand a full-time commitment to a lifestyle that includes regular practice activities. And there's another lesson we can learn from the practice habits of some, but not all, professional athletes. When describing this elite group you

Notes:

will hear this phrase: They play just as hard in practice as they do in the game. Observing how these elite athletes approach excellence inspires those around them to improve their own practice habits.

The true steward reflects a consistent lifestyle of generosity and giving in many areas of his or her life. They understand that it's not enough to give once and think their gift has fulfilled an obligation. As we take a look at the next five chapters covering Basic, Sacrificial, Extraordinary, Compassion, and Thanks Giving, we will come to understand how important it is for us to incorporate a pattern of giving and generosity into our lifestyles.

PRACTICE IS WELL-PACED

To be sustainable over a long period of time we need to maintain a pace that is neither too intense nor too lax. Practice that is too lax doesn't lead to improvement; practice that is too intense leads to burnout and abandoning the activity. Just as Goldilocks discovered when she tried out the three chairs, there was one that was too hard and one that was too soft. One was just right.

What does this have to do with giving? I've known of people who gave out of human emotion rather than responding to God's voice and wisdom. They gave too much too soon, like athletes overexerting themselves in practice. Unfortunately, the long-term impact of these kinds of gifts was not excellence in giving and generosity, but disillusionment. Emotional or guilt-induced giving can

Notes:

lead to abandoning the whole idea of generous living. What a shame.

But I've also known of another group—let's call them the underachievers. Their giving regimen was too lax. The result was that they never quite realized their potential. They coasted along in life well below the level of performance and excellence that could have been theirs. It can happen in all areas of life. What a shame.

However, Paul tells us not to be a part of either of these groups. He says to us that we should be, and can be, in a group that fulfills our potential and achieves excellence in generosity. As we discovered in chapter 12, the rewards experienced by the faithful steward can dwarf anything else that life has to offer.

PRACTICE OFTEN GOES UNRECOGNIZED

How true. We who sit in the stands and applaud have no real comprehension of and appreciation for the sacrifices that make great game performances possible. I can't imagine the mental disciplines required to be a distance runner and how many miles they run in solitude to prepare themselves for the big race.

I think few of us have any idea how much "practice" and sacrifice is involved in the lives of those who strive for excellence in generosity. And to the truly generous it doesn't matter. Their excellence in giving is not about recognition, it is about obedience. We'll talk more about this in chapter 24.

Notes:

PRACTICE IS NOT THE TIME FOR COMPARISONS

The purpose of practice is for each person to achieve the best levels of performance they possibly can. The only real point of comparison, then, is for each of us to judge our performance against our own potential. Are we doing all we can to achieve the levels of excellence that are possible for us? That's what matters.

Comparing what we do with what others do almost inevitably leads to reduced levels of performance. If I'm about to race someone that is obviously faster than I am, it's easy for me to think, *What's the use, I can't win,* and give up before I start. Or, if I'm the faster runner, there's always a tendency to run only fast enough to win, but not fast enough to do my best. The purpose of practice is for each of us to do his best with what he's been given. That's what a steward does.

PRACTICE BECOMES SECOND NATURE

This is very similar to practice becoming a lifestyle except that it goes one step further. When practice becomes second nature to us, we no longer have to think about it. Generosity becomes an automatic response to the events surrounding us.

Allow me to use another great golf illustration to demonstrate how the various aspects of practice translate into how we perform. Several years ago I watched a post-tournament interview with Tiger Woods, shortly after he won the prestigious Masters

Notes:

Tournament in Augusta, Georgia. When he was asked if there was a critical shot he made to ensure his victory, he didn't hesitate for a moment and his answer amazed me. His response was

> We learn that we can trust God, and God learns that He can trust us.
> 🌿

something like this: "I knew that the tee shot on the thirteenth hole would be crucial and I would need to hit a three wood from right to left around the corner of the fairway. For the past two and a half months I practiced the kind of shot I wanted to make there."

Two and a half months! For one shot! It still amazes me when I think about it, but it doesn't surprise me anymore. In the last few years, Tiger Woods has established a level of excellence among professional golfers that is unsurpassed, and it didn't happen by accident. It was intentional and it became second nature to him.

There is much we can learn about practice from the example of Tiger Woods.

- His practice was purposeful. He established a goal and specifically worked on those things in practice that would help him achieve the excellence he wanted.
- His practice involved repetition. How many practice sessions were involved, and how many swings did it take for Tiger to hit the shot he wanted? More than I can imagine, but enough to get the desired result.
- His practice reflected a lifestyle commitment to excellence. Players without the lifestyle commitment probably would

Notes:

have been satisfied with far less preparation and rewarded with far less success.

- His practice was measured at a pace designed for success. Hitting two practice shots a day, or two thousand practice shots on the day before the tournament, wasn't Tiger's plan. He paced his practice over a two-and-a-half-month period!

- His practice was about achieving excellence with his skills. I seriously doubt Tiger thought much about what anyone else would do when they arrived at the thirteenth hole. He concentrated on what he wanted to do, then did it.

- When Tiger arrived at the thirteenth tee he didn't think to himself, *Gee, I wonder what I'm supposed to do now?* This is a key point for the steward. Tiger knew because he was prepared and it was second nature to him. Standing over that tee shot was not the time to think about all of the mechanics of the golf swing: keep the head down, left arm straight, good shoulder turn, transfer the weight at impact, and so on. No, all of those things had been reviewed before he got there. When Tiger arrived on the thirteenth hole that day, he was successful because his preparation had given him a high level of confidence that what he wanted to do, he would be able to do.

When we strive for excellence, and seek to excel in the grace of giving by practicing and demonstrating generosity in the small things, two things happen. We learn that we can trust God, and God learns that He can trust us. That's a great combination, one

Notes:

that gives us confidence that God is able and willing to supply *through us* when He puts a larger challenge in our path.

A Prayer for Your Day

Heavenly Father, I ask You to let each of us experience the thrill that comes with excellence. May we be exhilarated at the accomplishment that You want to achieve through us. Prepare us for these moments. Place into our spirits a desire to achieve everything that You purpose for us. Place us in situations that require a generous response. Build our confidence that You are worthy of our trust and that we will trust You. Your work is always excellent; bring us to that place where our desire is to be excellent as well, because that is Your plan for us. Amen.

❦

Reflect & Respond

List some areas of your life where you excel.

Consider whether these areas of excellence were accidental or intentional.

Consider how striving to "excel in this grace of giving" can have a positive impact in the discipline of your finances.

CHAPTER SIXTEEN

Basic Giving

Mastering the basics is absolutely essential.

❦

A tithe of everything from the land, whether grain from the soil or
fruit from the trees, belongs to the LORD; it is holy to the LORD.

—LEVITICUS 27:30

I'm sure the mere thought of giving 10 percent of your income as an offering each month, what the Bible calls *the tithe,* is enough to scare many of you to death. In this chapter I'm going to do my best to explain why it shouldn't.

Yes, I'm aware of the federal, state, sometimes local, disability, social security, Medicare, and other miscellaneous taxes that already shrink your paycheck. I pay them too. So this is not a hypothetical chapter written from an ivory tower somewhere in fantasyland. It's grounded solidly in a steward's reality. Giving 10 percent can be absolutely the best financial decision you'll ever make. I promise. Much better, it's a promise that God makes to you.

Malachi 3:10 says, "Bring your full tithe to the Temple treasury so there will be ample provisions in my Temple. Test me in this and see if I don't open up heaven itself to you and pour out blessings beyond your wildest dreams" (MSG). If that's not a promise, I don't know what is. "Test me in this and see...." See what? See if He doesn't respond in ways we could never imagine.

That can be part of the problem for us, though, the fact that the tithe involves a blessing that is beyond our wildest dreams, something we can't begin to imagine. Because our minds tend to process logically rather than spiritually, it's difficult for us to believe that if we give 10 percent, we can live better with what we have left. How is it possible for us to do better financially by having 10 percent less, especially when so many of us are already swamped by bills? Trust me when I say that I understand the difficulty in grasping this concept, but it's true. My prayer is that you'll see the truth of what Malachi says, act on it in obedience, and experience the tremendous opportunity (blessing) that he describes. Whatever it takes for us to experience this truth is worth the effort and, like I've said before, what do you have to lose? Maybe it's time to "test [God] in this and see."

> **It is no small thing to align your finances with God's purposes.**
> ❧

For centuries people have trusted, tested, and testified to the truth of the tithe. We can learn from them. I can't tell you how many times I've heard someone describe their financial turn-around in words like these:

Financially we were a complete disaster. We avoided answering the phone because we didn't know what to tell the collectors.

Notes:

We were out of control with no hope that it could ever get better. Then we heard about tithing. At first it didn't make sense but the more we considered it, the more we realized that nothing about the way we were already handling our finances made any sense either. We figured why not? There was nothing to lose and if the Bible was right, we had a lot to gain. We started faithfully giving 10 percent. It was the best thing we ever did and we can't imagine ever going back to managing our finances the way we did before.

What changed? Everything. How did it happen? In several ways. First and foremost, God stepped in. That's how He responds to our obedience and it's impossible to overestimate the value of His help. It's no small thing to align your finances with God's purposes. But there are some other factors at work here too.

In the process of teaching stewardship principles in various churches, I've occasionally been asked this question: "We're hopelessly in debt. How can we afford to tithe? Won't committing to tithe just make our situation worse?" My answer has always been to focus on the principles involved and not the circumstances. I ask questions like, "Are your financial troubles the result of following biblical stewardship principles, or are they the result of following the counsel of our consumer-driven culture?" I've yet to have anyone respond that their problems resulted from following biblical principles. That leads to a follow-up question: "If

Notes:

avoiding biblical principles of stewardship created your problems, will continuing to ignore biblical principles solve them?" Not likely!

There's a dynamic involved when cultural consumerism guides our spending and finances. That dynamic is a lack of financial discipline. Buy. Spend. New. Big. *Now!* Tithing, on the other hand, represents a commitment in the opposite direction. For many people, it's the first time in their adult lives they've exercised financial discipline in anything, and that discipline can be contagious. People who change their thinking and decide to give 10 percent regularly are people who can change their thinking in other areas as well. Before too long they find themselves in control of their finances instead of being victimized by them.

We need to stop right here to think about what that means. The implications are *huge!* Think about the sense of relief and freedom that is released in the homes of those who move from a lifestyle of "our finances control us" to "we control our finances." The siege mentality is gone! When we get a glimpse of the joy and happiness that come with this radical transformation, then we'll understand why the tithing story we read earlier in this chapter is always shared by a smiling face. Always!

A commitment to tithe also opens us to an understanding of the truths in other Bible references about basic giving principles. Consider the following four passages.

- "Honor the LORD with your wealth and with the best
  part of everything your land produces." (Proverbs 3:9, NLT)

Notes:

- "Celebrate … by giving a freewill offering in proportion to the blessings the LORD your God has given you." (Deuteronomy 16:10)
- "On the first day of the week, each one of you should set aside a sum of money in keeping with his income." (1 Corinthians 16:2)
- "Hypocrites! For you are careful to tithe even the tiniest part of your income, but you ignore the important things of the law—justice, mercy, and faith. You should tithe, yes, but you should not leave undone the more important things." (Matthew 23:23, NLT)

We need to learn the principles of these references. They can make all the difference in the world in how we regard and manage our money and possessions.

HONOR THE LORD

Sometimes the best way to consider something is to imagine its absence. Let's do that. How would we describe a person who was given access to a steward's resources (chapter 9), was equipped with valuable talents and gifts (chapter 7), and understood he was not limited by natural realities (chapter 11)—and in response to this did nothing? Had no gratitude. No thanks. No honor. I don't know about you, but that's not the kind of person I want to be around. When we give 10 percent we acknowledge God's role in our lives and we honor Him for what He has done for us. How can we do any less?

Notes:

GIVE THE BEST PART

There's a too-common mind-set among some people that I call the Junk-for-Jesus syndrome. They don't give the best part to ministry, they give the leftovers, the stuff that no longer has value to them. The Bible says this attitude is backwards. God deserves the best part, so make your tithe the first check you write, not the last. It's more than a symbolic gesture, it's a reflection of priorities.

CELEBRATE

Imagine for a moment that as a parent you did something really special for your daughter. Shortly thereafter the phone rings or there's a knock on the front door. It's your daughter almost bursting with joy. She's got a smile that could light the darkest depression. She's overflowing with energy and excitement. She has a simple message: *thanks.* That's all, just thanks. But, oh, the way the thanks was given elevates the word from an expression to an immeasurable treasure. How long has it been since you celebrated God's goodness in your giving? Why not bring the joy to Him in that same childlike way?

SHARE IN PROPORTION

I love this aspect of giving because it levels the playing field. Our gifts are not measured against the millionaire's, but against the income that we have. Each of us is called to share proportionally

Notes:

in our sacrifice. None of us gains any standing or stature with God because we have more to give. Isn't that just like God? Even in our ability to give back to him He finds a way for us all to be equal in His sight. I love it!

GIVE WEEKLY

Pam and I were married in 1970. You can do the math to figure out how long we've been married. On that great day in June all those years ago, I said "I love you" to my new bride, but we all know it's not smart to go very long between saying it again. I think that bringing our tithe weekly is a way of frequently saying "I love you" to God. The actual process of regularly writing the tithe check is an act of commitment and sacrifice. I didn't always tithe this way but since I started to tithe weekly, giving has become much more meaningful to me.

REMEMBER THAT IT'S ABOUT MORE THAN JUST MONEY

In chapter 13 we saw how Saul learned that God values obedience more than He does sacrifice. One way or the other we'll learn that too. "Yes, you should tithe," Matthew quotes Jesus as telling the religious leaders. But he tells them, and us, that the tithe does not discharge our obligation to more important things such as seeking justice and mercy. We'll look more at this giving in chapter 19.

The decision to give 10 percent can change not just your

Notes:

finances but your entire life as you invite God to join you on a Steward's Journey. I encourage you to make that decision. What do you have to lose?

True stewards don't look for legal loopholes in a contract that would release them from an obligation to God. True stewards look through the lens of opportunity for ways to fulfill a covenant with God. Remember, it's important to tithe because it opens God's blessing to us. But giving money is not enough. True stewards look for a closer relationship with God, and that requires obedience as well as sacrifice. I urge you not to be distant from Him. Come closer to Him. Test Him. See how He blesses you in return.

A Prayer for Your Day

Heavenly Father, You promise in Your Word to give blessings to those who are faithful in giving their tithe to You. As I pray right now, I am aware that for many people reading these pages, giving a tithe doesn't make sense. They have too little already and they aren't certain what to do next. I am asking You to help them trust. I am asking You to help them make this decision to follow Your plan for their lives. Others already know that You are worthy of our trust and join me in asking that You grant the full measure of blessing into the lives of those who are about to trust You for the first time. Thanks for being faithful to them. Amen.

❧

REFLECT & RESPOND

Study your check register and credit card statements to review your spending for the past two months. What do your financial habits say about your life priorities?

Pray for wisdom to know how to reorder your spending habits so that they reflect the life priorities of a faithful steward.

Malachi 3:10 says, "Bring the whole tithe into the storehouse, that there may be food in my house. Test me in this," says the LORD Almighty, "and see if I will not throw open the floodgates of heaven and pour out so much blessing that you will not have room enough for it." Test Him. You will see.

CHAPTER SEVENTEEN

Sacrificial Giving

Any offering of consequence has a price tag.

❦

No, I insist on buying it, for I cannot present burnt
offerings to the LORD my God that have cost me nothing.
—2 SAMUEL 24:24, NLT

I'm not sure about you, but sacrifice doesn't come easy for me. It never has. By its very definition the concept of sacrifice carries a price tag because it means we have to *give up something*. Sometimes sacrifice involves our money, at other times it's about not getting our way. Regardless, real sacrifice is always costly.

I have to laugh when I think back to what was probably my first encounter with the concept of sacrifice. I was nine years old and in my first year of Little League baseball when the coach taught us about the sacrifice bunt. If you're not familiar with baseball terms, the sacrifice bunt is when the batter deliberately hits the ball only far enough to advance his teammates one base but in the process he usually makes an out at first base. It's a fascinating process to watch, and a bitter pill to swallow for some young and not-so-young batters who see themselves as home-run hitters. When a player returns to the dugout, he wants to do it with the glory of driving in runs, not in the less glamorous role of moving runners into scoring position for others to drive in. I'm sure any kid who's played baseball for a number of years can remember a teammate who simply refused to sacrifice himself with a bunt. They'd disguise their refusal with halfhearted attempts to bunt or with bunts that deliberately went foul. These kids weren't about to sacrifice themselves, not when they could swing away and try to be the game-winning hero. They were, and still are, almost too comical to watch, with transparent motives so obvious that they don't fool anyone, especially their teammates.

We can find those who are unwilling to sacrifice on virtually any team in almost any endeavor. Think about your own experience. Haven't we all known someone who wasn't willing to pay the price and give up his or her will, way, or money? But giving something up is exactly what we are called to do on the occasions when we are called to give sacrificially.

Scripture places a high value on sacrificial giving and we'll look at a few examples in just a minute. As I'm writing this, though, I'm struck by some of the ways our culture also values the concept of sacrifice, and I'd like to illustrate this with some everyday examples.

First, think about how you would respond if two friends remembered your birthday with gifts, but each gift held different meaning based on what you know about the unique financial circumstances of your friends. Let's say the first friend gave you a fairly expensive and nicely gift-wrapped package. From past experience you know that this friend doesn't have to worry about money. For your second

Notes:

friend, though, finding enough money to buy a nice gift wasn't as easy. The second friend took the time to make something for you—your favorite cookies, a bouquet of fresh flowers, or a handcrafted gift for the home. The value of this gift was measured more in time and thought than in money. Isn't there something about the sacrificial nature of the second gift that automatically increases its value in our minds?

> **When sacrifice is involved, the value of the *gift* increases even while the value of the *object* remains the same.**

Stop and consider this: when sacrifice is involved, the value of the *gift* increases even while the value of the *object* remains the same. Here's what I mean: as *objects*, two $100 gift certificates have the same value. But if we know one was purchased with a virtually unlimited bank account and the other was purchased only after months of saving and going without, aren't we likely to value the second gift certificate more highly?

Here's another way to think about how much the element of sacrifice can add or detract from the value of a gift. Suppose the first gift we talked about earlier was something quite expensive, something we really wanted and were very appreciative to receive, but it was also pricey enough to make us a bit self-conscious at how much money our friend spent. Maybe we might try to ease our concern by commenting, "You really shouldn't have spent this much on me." But I wonder how our feelings would change if our friend responded, "Oh, don't worry about it. Someone gave me

Notes:

several and I had an extra." Wouldn't it diminish the value of the gift if something like that happened? Why? Because without some measure of sacrifice in the gift, it goes from being something special to something surplus. Think for a moment about whether that has been true in your own experience.

In the book of Mark, Jesus tells a story that highlights the importance of sacrifice in our giving: "Jesus sat down opposite the place where the offerings were put and watched the crowd putting their money into the temple treasury. Many rich people threw in large amounts. But a poor widow came and put in two very small copper coins, worth only a fraction of a penny" (12:41-42). As you read Jesus' observation about the widow's gift in the verses that follow, keep in mind that there are very few gifts in the history of the world that are as well known as the widow's mite. Yet we don't even know her name and we know nothing about her life except that she was beyond poor. In fact, if Jesus hadn't observed what the widow gave that day, it's certain that no one else would have noticed, especially compared to the much more sizable donations that the wealthier people were making at the same time. But Jesus noticed and He had this to say: "The truth is that this poor widow gave more to the collection than all the others put together. All the others gave what they'll never miss; she gave extravagantly what she couldn't afford—she gave her all" (Mark 12:43-44, MSG).

Measured in today's money, the value of her offering was probably less than a penny. But measured in terms of sacrifice her offering was extraordinarily valuable. Twenty centuries later it is

Notes:

still taught as an example of sacrificial giving and is probably known by hundreds of millions of people around the world today. Why? Because man typically honors the *size of the gift,* but God always honors the *size of the sacrifice.*

I'd like us to concentrate on four key points about sacrificial giving from the story of the widow's gift.

- Sacrificial gifts aren't given from our surplus. This was certainly the case for the widow because she gave all she had. This means that on those occasions when we are called to give sacrificially, it will require more than writing an additional check after all of our normal monthly bills are paid, or withdrawing from our saving accounts while we continue to live life as usual.

- Sacrificial gifts change priorities. In chapter 5 we discussed the idea that for every yes there's a no. When the widow said yes to the offering she gave, it meant she could only say no to anything else the mite could have been used for. By giving all she had, the widow showed that she valued the act of giving more than she valued what she could acquire with her money.

- Sacrificial gifts are honored by God. Think about the unique honor given by God to the widow in this story. She wasn't rich enough to get her name on a building or engraved on an ornate plaque in the lobby. We don't know her name, but God does. He noticed and brought honor to an otherwise insignificant giver and gift.

Notes:

• Sacrificial gifts inspire others. I don't think there's any
doubt that the widow's example has inspired many others to
give sacrificially in the past two thousand years. I've also
personally observed the impact of modern day sacrificial
giving and how it inspires others to live more generously.

Before we leave the subject of sacrificial giving, there's no better example than what Paul shares in the second chapter of his letter to the Philippians.

> Think of yourselves the way Christ Jesus thought of himself.
> He had equal status with God but didn't think so much of
> himself that he had to cling to the advantages of that status no
> matter what. Not at all. When the time came, he set aside the
> privileges of deity and took on the status of a slave, became
> human! Having become human, he stayed human. It was an
> incredibly humbling process. He didn't claim special privileges.
> Instead he lived a selfless, obedient life and then died a selfless,
> obedient death—and the worst kind of death at that: a crucifix-
> ion. (verses 5-8, MSG)

Look at what Jesus did in terms of sacrificial giving, and what
He voluntarily gave up in the process. Here's the price tag on His
gift to us:

• He had equal status with God but determined that there
    was something valuable enough for which to sacrifice this
    status.

Notes:

- He had all the privileges of deity, but He voluntarily set those aside in order to experience the human condition with mankind and communicate God's message to us.
- Then, as if that weren't enough, He voluntarily accepted a violent, terrible, and humiliating end to His human life. He did these things as God's way of giving us a gift, a gift of the highest value because it was given at the highest cost.

The implications of Jesus' sacrificial gift in our lives are staggering to consider. Think about the incredible value each of us must have in God's eyes since He was willing to pay such an unbelievable price for our return to Him. Here's another way to illustrate the principle. If you've ever sold a house you know that, ultimately, the value of a house is not established by your realtor nor by the recent sale prices of other homes in your neighborhood. No, the value of a house, and really the value of anything, is determined by what someone else is willing to pay for it. It only takes one interested and highly motivated buyer to sell a house. In real estate, if someone wants a house badly enough, they'll pay the price. This principle applies to us, too. Ultimately our value is established in Christ's sacrifice for us.

If we've ever had doubts about our worth or our value, the sacrifice described in Philippians 2 should forever put them to rest. We are unbelievably valuable because God paid an unbelievable price for our safe return to Him. We are worth what has been paid for us, and the price that was paid is the most amazing demonstration of sacrificial giving ever.

Notes:

Let's review the Bible reference at the beginning of this chapter: "No, I insist on buying it, for I cannot present burnt offerings to the LORD my God that have cost me nothing" (2 Samuel 24:24, NLT). The reference is from an event that took place approximately nine hundred years before the birth of Christ, when David demonstrated the connection between sacrifice and truly meaningful giving. Here's more background from that story:

> Araunah looked up and saw David and his men coming his way; he met them, bowing deeply, honoring the king and saying, "Why has my master the king come to see me?"
>
> "To buy your threshing floor," said David, "so I can build an altar to GOD here and put an end to this disaster." "Oh," said Araunah, "let my master the king take and sacrifice whatever he wants. Look, here's an ox for the burnt offering and threshing paddles and ox-yokes for fuel—Araunah gives it all to the king! And may GOD, your God, act in your favor.
>
> But the king said to Araunah, "No. I've got to buy it from you for a good price; I'm not going to offer GOD, my God, sacrifices that are no sacrifice." (2 Samuel 24:20-24, MSG)

It's not easy for us modern American consumers, who are always on the lookout for the best bargains and sales prices, to relate to someone paying more than a minimum price or market value. I suspect if we were in David's sandals we'd have accepted Araunah's offer, but that's not the way of a steward. There are

Notes:

times that require sacrifice and God can use these times to have us examine and reorder our spending and life priorities. These are the times when we can invest our lives in a cause greater than ourselves, and times that can reshape our hearts into valuing those things that are close to God's heart. Frankly, as we'll see in the chapter on Thanks Giving, there is a strong connection between our ability to give sacrificially and our understanding of how much Christ sacrificed for us. Right now, though, I'd like to pray for each of us to understand that connection more clearly than we ever have before, and ask each of us to spend some time thinking about a lifestyle that makes room for sacrifice.

A Prayer for Your Day

Heavenly Father, no matter how much we think we can understand what You have done for us, it is beyond our comprehension. Teach us more, though, than what we know now. Open our eyes, hearts, and minds to a greater understanding of what Your sacrifice means to us and what our sacrifice can mean to others. Use sacrifice to teach us more about You and about us. Bring us to the point where we no longer measure sacrifice in terms of cost but in terms of blessing. Thank You that You are able to make this happen. Amen.

REFLECT & RESPOND

Reflect on your personal experiences with sacrificial giving, either as the one who made sacrifices or the one who benefited from them.

How did you feel about these experiences at the time and have your feelings changed over time?

Consider whether there are those you know who are known to be sacrificial givers. Describe other characteristics of their lives.

Consider whether or not there are things in your life that need to be sacrificed in order for you to be a better steward of your resources.

CHAPTER EIGHTEEN

Extraordinary Giving

There are seasons for every church and believer
when extraordinary giving is required.

❧

*So Moses gave the command, and this message was
sent throughout the camp: "Bring no more materials!
You have already given more than enough."*

—EXODUS 36:6, NLT

The graphic combat scenes of the amphibious assault on French beaches in the opening minutes of *Saving Private Ryan* changed the way moviegoers view the ugly realities of war. But it was a combination of both the film's opening and closing scenes, featuring the solemn reflection of an elderly private Ryan surrounded by neat rows of headstones in a Normandy bluffs cemetery, that captured the essence of extraordinary giving for me. Overwhelmed with memories of the past, a living private Ryan stands at the grave of a fallen Captain John H. Miller and says, "I hope that, at least in your eyes, I've earned what all of you have done for me."

The summer before my senior year in high school I visited Arlington National Cemetery for the first time, and it was truly an unforgettable experience. Arlington's two hundred acres of land contain more than a quarter million grave sites. This seventeen year-old southern Californian with so little life experience was very definitely out of place among the nation's founders and defenders, from privates to presidents. I've been fortunate enough to visit Arlington several more times since that occasion and each time I gain a bit more perspective for the sacrifices represented there. Each time I take away a greater sense of personal responsibility to properly acknowledge and be a good steward of the extraordinary gifts that are now mine because of those sacrifices. Like the elder private Ryan, in my own way I'm trying to earn what others have done for me and, in turn, leave the mark of my own sacrifice for those who will follow.

In our nation's history there have been seasons when its citizens have been called upon to give extraordinarily. For every church and believer there are also seasons when extraordinary giving is required. Our discussion today is about the seasons on a Steward's Journey that require extraordinary giving.

Accounting practices make a distinction between operating and capital expenses. Operating expenses generally involve the routine conduct of daily business and include such things as salaries, rent, sales and marketing, and the costs associated with developing products and services. Capital expenditures are less frequent but their impact is longer lasting. Businesses may need to make capital expenditures to upgrade their information systems to remain competitive in the future because past investments are no longer sufficient to meet the growing demands for reliable

Notes:

and actionable information. Another example is plant expansion, when a business has simply outgrown the manufacturing capacity of its existing facilities and needs to purchase more land and construct new factories. Annual operating budgets that reflect normal income and expenses are not sufficient to finance these capital needs.

Churches and ministries have the same challenges. At least those that are vibrant and growing do. What does a church do when it reaches the capacity of its existing facilities and its future growth is threatened by the lack of classroom space, sanctuary seating, or family recreation capabilities? The normal sources of income, tithes, and sacrificial giving are not enough to continue existing ministries and fund the necessary new facilities at the same time. These are the seasons when extraordinary giving is required, and there are two primary examples in the Bible that can guide our understanding of it.

Let's set the scene for the example recorded in the book of Exodus beginning in chapter 25 but primarily in chapters 35 and 36. After more than 400 years of slavery and increasing oppression at the hands of the Egyptians, Moses has finally succeeded in leading Israel out of Egypt. It's hard for me to imagine the scene: over 600,000 men, not counting women and children, encamped in the rugged desert wilderness near Mount Sinai. And don't forget the livestock. The organizational challenge was huge. Two months have passed and many encounters with God have taken place since Israel left Egypt only to find themselves in what was essentially an

Notes:

ancient refugee camp on a massive scale. This was the setting when the Ten Commandments were given. Moses also received many other instructions and among these was specific direction to build a place for God to live among them: "I want the people of Israel to build me a sacred residence where I can live among them. You must make this Tabernacle and its furnishings exactly according to the plans I will show you" (Exodus 25:8-9, NLT).

The families and tribes of Israel had been making their normal sacrifices in the routine activities of life but now they were faced with a new need: a dwelling place for God built to His specifications. The financing plan was a very simple one and didn't involve bonds, borrowing, or brokers. Listen to the beginning of the chapter from the *New Living Translation:* "The LORD said to Moses, 'Tell the people of Israel that everyone who wants to may bring me an offering. Here is a list of items you may accept on my behalf: gold, silver, and bronze; blue, purple, and scarlet yarn; fine linen; goat hair for cloth; tanned ram skins and fine goatskin leather; acacia wood; olive oil for the lamps; spice for the anointing oil and the fragrant incense; onyx stones, and other stones to be set in the ephod and the chestpiece'" (Exodus 25:1-7).

Read the first part again: "Tell the people of Israel that *everyone who wants to* may bring me an offering." Extraordinary giving is voluntary, not compulsory! If we want to we *may.* Those of you who've had the opportunity to review legal documents understand the significance of the word "may" as opposed to the word "shall." It's as if even in the selection of the language given to

Notes:

Moses, God stresses the importance of the willingness of those who bring their gifts. Even in these early examples of giving we are reminded that God loves the cheerful giver; He loves it when the giver delights in the giving.

After ten chapters in Exodus that primarily involve the detailed planning for the tabernacle and its operation, Moses returns to the subject of offerings in chapters 35 and 36. In case anyone had forgotten the voluntary nature of extraordinary giving, he drives the point home with these references in chapter 35: *everyone who is willing* (verse 5), *everyone who was willing and whose heart moved him* (verse 21), *all who were willing, men and women alike* (verse 22), *all the women who were willing* (verse 26), *all the Israelite men and women who were willing* (verse 29). The theme continues into chapter 36: *and every skilled person to whom the LORD had given ability and who was willing to come* (verse 2), *and the people continued to bring freewill offerings morning after morning* (verse 3).

An interesting thing happened as the people voluntarily and extraordinarily gave. They had enough or, to be more precise, they had more than enough.

> So all the skilled craftsmen who were doing all the work on the sanctuary left their work and said to Moses, "The people are bringing more than enough for doing the work the LORD commanded to be done." Then Moses gave an order and they sent this word throughout the camp: "No man or woman is to make

Notes:

anything else as an offering for the sanctuary." And so the people were restrained from bringing more, because what they already had was more than enough to do all the work. (Exodus 36:4-7)

Imagine your pastor making that kind of pulpit announcement in response to an extraordinary response to a huge need in your church!

There's an interesting side note I like to remember here. Israel had only recently escaped Egyptian slavery. Where did they get many of the valuable offerings they presented to God at Sinai? The answer is found in Exodus 12:35-36:

And the people of Israel did as Moses had instructed and asked the Egyptians for clothing and articles of silver and gold. The LORD caused the Egyptians to look favorably on the Israelites, and they gave the Israelites whatever they asked for. So, like a victorious army, they plundered the Egyptians! (NLT)

Even after four hundred years of want, the Israelites where willing to share their newly acquired and God-provided abundance when extraordinary giving was required.

Let me share one more great aspect of this story before we move on to the second example. Notice the list of items that Moses could accept on behalf of God. It contained items of great value like gold and silver, and also things like acacia wood and

---

Notes:

goat hair that, humanly speaking, don't have the same perceived value. I love the fact that in this example God clearly shows us that there is something that each of us can bring when we're involved with seasons of extraordinary giving. We may not have gold and silver but our sweat and labor can bring a harvest of acacia wood. God assigns the true value of the offering, not man. In His sight there's acceptance in both the silver and the goat hair. Each of us has something we can bring if we are willing!

> God assigns the true value of the offering, not man.
> ❦

Let's briefly look at a second example of extraordinary giving found in 1 Chronicles 29. This Old Testament reference forms the pattern followed by many churches today that conduct capital stewardship campaigns to assist them with their capital financing needs.

In this example, King David wanted to supply provisions for his son, Solomon, to construct a temple in Jerusalem. *The Message* recounts the story like this in the first nine verses of chapter 29:

> Then David the king addressed the congregation: "My son
> Solomon was singled out and chosen by God to do this. But
> he's young and untested and the work is huge—this is not just
> a place for people to meet each other, but a house for God to
> meet us. I've done my best to get everything together for build-
> ing this house for my God, all the materials necessary: gold,

Notes:

silver, bronze, iron, lumber, precious and varicolored stones, and building stones—vast stockpiles. Furthermore, because my heart is in this, in addition to and beyond what I have gathered, I'm turning over my personal fortune of gold and silver for making this place of worship for my God.... And now, how about you? Who among you is ready and willing to join in the giving?" Ready and willing, the heads of families, leaders of the tribes of Israel, commanders and captains in the army, stewards of the king's affairs, stepped forward and gave willingly... Anyone who had precious jewels put them in the treasury for the building of the Temple of God.... And the people were full of a sense of celebration—all that giving! And all given willingly, freely! King David was exuberant.

As was the case of the building of the tabernacle, the provisions offered for the building of the temple were brought willingly. There is no room for coercion or reluctance when God's Spirit calls His stewards to give extraordinarily. David set the example and challenged his leaders. The leaders responded with such enthusiasm that all of Israel celebrated and participated. It was a wonderful demonstration of stewardship in action, for an extraordinary time.

Consider this final thought as we close the chapter. Each of us benefits from the sacrifices of those who have purchased the freedom we enjoy, built the churches where we worship, taught us the responsibilities of citizenship, and instructed us in the character

---

Notes:

and ways of God. It is up to us to be good stewards of what we've been given and ensure an equal or greater heritage for those who follow us. In a song made famous by Steve Green, songwriter Jon Mohr captured the spirit of the steward with these words: "May all who come behind us find us faithful." May they, indeed.

That was what the elderly private Ryan was seeking when he returned to the Normandy cemetery as an old man. He wanted to be faithful to the extraordinary sacrifices that had made his life possible. If each of us on a Steward's Journey had a similar goal, to honor the sacrifices of those who went before us with extraordinary giving of our own, the world, the future, and the kingdom would be so much better for it.

A Prayer for Your Day

Heavenly Father, help us to respond extraordinarily when we are faced with the opportunity to do so, and may our response be cheerfully given and not from obligation. Help us understand all the ways that we benefit from the gifts of those who came before us and give us a vision of the impact our gifts can have on those in the future. May those who follow us examine our actions and say that we were good stewards of our heritage and our legacy. Amen.

REFLECT & RESPOND

If you've experienced a time in your life when long-term giving was required, describe how you responded and the impact it had on you.

How do you respond when you hear about the extraordinary gifts others have made?

List some of the things you can do now to help you prepare for making a commitment to give extraordinarily.

If possible, arrange to speak with someone you know and trust who has experienced extraordinary giving. Let them tell you the impact it had on their life and ask them to pray with you for future opportunities in your life.

CHAPTER NINETEEN

Compassion Giving

Live in such a way that thanksgiving
follows wherever you've been.

❦

Share with God's people who are in need. Practice hospitality.
—ROMANS 12:13

A dictionary definition of compassion says "the humane quality of understanding the suffering of others and wanting to do something about it." James makes a connection between this compassion and what God views as pure and lasting religion when he says it "means that we must care for orphans and widows in their troubles" (James 1:27, NLT). Good stewards *practice hospitality and share with God's people who are in need.* The Scripture tells us about some who shared and others who did not.

"Not everyone passed by on the other side." If you grew up in the church the chances are fairly good that you know the Bible passage I'm referencing. But in case you don't remember or have never heard the story, let me share how Luke recorded it.

A Jewish man was traveling on a trip from Jerusalem to Jericho,
and he was attacked by bandits. They stripped him of his

clothes and money, beat him up, and left him half dead beside the road. By chance a Jewish priest came along; but when he saw the man lying there, he crossed to the other side of the road and passed him by. A Temple assistant walked over and looked at him lying there, but he also passed by on the other side. Then a despised Samaritan came along, and when he saw the man, he felt deep pity. Kneeling beside him, the Samaritan soothed his wounds with medicine and bandaged them. Then he put the man on his own donkey and took him to an inn, where he took care of him. The next day he handed the innkeeper two pieces of silver and told him to take care of the man. 'If his bill runs higher than that,' he said, 'I'll pay the difference the next time I am here.' Now which of these three would you say was a neighbor to the man who was attacked by bandits?" Jesus asked. The man replied, "The one who showed him mercy." Then Jesus said, "Yes, now go and do the same." (Luke 10:30-37, NLT)

This story was one of the first I can remember hearing as a child and I still recall why it was unusual. It's because the mercy was shown by the one who was the least likely of the three to demonstrate such compassion, the despised good Samaritan. The priest or the Levite (temple assistant) should have responded with compassion, but they didn't. Only the hated Samaritan responded compassionately to what he came across on the Jericho road that day.

If we take a close look at what Scripture says Compassion Giving

---

Notes:

means to God, I think we'll discover that it's hard to overstate its importance. I also think we'll see that Compassion Giving isn't an optional "multiple choice" decision that's just one of many giving alternatives. No! Compassion Giving is no less an option for the good steward than it was for the good Samaritan, because caring for the less fortunate and those in need is an issue that is constantly near God's heart. How do we know that? By looking at how Jesus treated the unfortunate.

During the three years of Jesus' public ministry, He was constantly meeting the needs of others. Inevitably the stories of His teaching and miracles preceded Him wherever He went, and often caused Him to be greeted by crowds demanding even more. Look at how Matthew describes Jesus' typical response: "When he saw the crowds, he had compassion on them, because they were harassed and helpless" (Matthew 9:36). Mark adds these words of Jesus,

> **Caring for the less fortunate is an issue that is constantly near God's heart.**
> ❧

following three days when he'd taught thousands of His followers: "I have compassion for these people; they have already been with me three days and have nothing to eat" (Mark 8:2). Even during the occasions when He needed time away from the crowds to rest physically or the time He wanted to be alone to grieve over the death of John the Baptist, a heart of compassion brought Him back to meeting the needs of the people: "As soon as Jesus heard the news [of John's death], he went off by himself in a boat to a

Notes:

remote area to be alone. But the crowds heard where he was headed and followed by land from many villages. A vast crowd was there as he stepped from the boat, and he had compassion on them and healed their sick" (Matthew 14:13-14, NLT). These references clearly reveal the compassion of Christ and some of the ways He expressed it.

One of my favorite Scripture references is found in the book of Hebrews: "The Son is the radiance of God's glory and the exact representation of his being" (Hebrews 1:3). *The Message* translates the verse like this: "This Son perfectly mirrors God, and is stamped with God's nature." If Jesus is the exact representation and perfect mirror of what God is like, it means that when we see what Jesus did on earth we gain a glimpse into God's heart. James describes God as being "full of compassion and mercy" (5:11). "The righteous care about justice for the poor," Proverbs 29:7, is one of many verses in Proverbs on the subject. God's concern for, and identification with, the poor is found in this passage: "He who is kind to the poor lends to the LORD" (Proverbs 19:17). And this reference not only commends our kindness to the poor but it also condemns our behaviors which take advantage of them: "You insult your Maker when you exploit the powerless; when you're kind to the poor, you honor God" (Proverbs 14:31, MSG). Finally, Proverbs connects our good stewardship in taking care of the poor with His provision for us: "He who gives to the poor will lack nothing" (Proverbs 28:27).

The interesting thing about all of these proverbs is that they're

---

Notes:

not merely historical references. They're guidelines for us in the present, and challenges for us to be better stewards of the resources God has entrusted to our management. Sometimes I wonder, though, what grade we would receive in the subject of Compassion Giving if we got report cards on our stewardship. Think about that as we consider a few examples of Compassion Giving.

In America the Salvation Army is best known for bell-ringers and collection kettles during the Christmas holidays. But in more than one hundred countries around the world, people see a different side of the organization. Energized by its mission to advance the cause of Christ, the Salvation Army operates homes for children, the elderly, the disabled, and the blind; they give medical treatment in their hospitals, clinics, and community health centers; and they serve the disadvantaged in life-changing activities including vocational education, prisoner rehabilitation, and addiction recovery programs. And they do much more. The Salvation Army doesn't cross by on the other side and leave society's wounded for others to treat.

Neither did Mother Teresa. Hers is perhaps the most recognizable face of compassion of the past century. Compassion took her from the comfortable environment of her European home, to a highly structured Catholic school regimen in India, to the chaotic and impoverished slums of Calcutta. Even after her death, her example and work continues around the world through those she inspired.

Truthfully, though, it's not the distant or institutional examples

---

Notes:

of Compassion Giving that are what this chapter is all about. This chapter is about personalizing Compassion Giving and incorporating it into the way we live. I remember a humbling and meaningful experience a number of years ago when money was scarce and bills were plentiful. One Sunday morning after church, a widow in her late 50s mentioned to Pam and me that she had several bags of groceries in her car that she had bought for us. This thoughtful woman's gift has come to represent the essence of Compassion Giving for us. It wasn't the sacrifice of a widow's mite because she wasn't, as far as we knew, in difficult financial circumstances. But her gift was the result of a compassionate heart, a gift from a person who sensed our need and responded to meet it. Pam remembers thinking (and saying) that we weren't in a position to repay her and the woman responded that repayment wasn't expected or necessary. "There will come a time, in the future, when you can pass this gift on to others." Since that time, we've been able to share compassionately with others in their times of need, and I must tell you that they've been some of the most meaningful moments of our lives.

Compassion Giving comes in many forms. In a moment I'm going to ask you to stop for a moment and reflect about how you've experienced it and the impact it has had on your life.

We know people who were done raising their own families, only to be confronted with the needs of other children, and through either adoption or foster parenting, made a place in their hearts and empty nests for them.

Notes:

We know men and women who consider the best week of their year to be when they give up five days of their vacations to work with abused, neglected, and abandoned children in a wonderful program called Royal Family Kids' Camps (www.rfkc.org).

We know those who set aside their time and money every week to prepare and serve meals to those who would otherwise go hungry.

We know tutors who work with both children and adults in order for them to become more proficient in their language or life skills so they will have a better chance for financial success.

We are better because we know these people of compassion.

Compassion Giving ensures that our hearts stay tender because it keeps us in touch with the needs around us. After all, we must be aware of needs before we can respond to them. That's why self-centered people aren't usually known for compassion; they are generally unaware of the real needs of others.

> Good stewards don't just give with their minds, they give with their hearts.
> 🌿

Good stewards don't just give with their minds, they give with their hearts. They give because they are keenly aware of needs and also of the reward that can be theirs by helping satisfy the need. Mother Teresa gave this advice: "Speak tenderly to them. Let there be kindness in your face, in your eyes, in your smile, in the warmth of your greeting. Always have a cheerful smile. Don't only give your care, but give your heart as well."

Notes:

Jesus also gave advice on the subject of Compassion Giving and I've saved it for the end of the chapter to emphasize its importance: "When you help someone out, don't think about how it looks. Just do it—quietly and unobtrusively. That is the way your God, who conceived you in love, working behind the scenes, helps you out" (Matthew 6:3-4, MSG). Compassion Giving doesn't seek the spotlight, it's content to remain behind the scenes. It's done "quietly and unobtrusively" out of respect for the dignity of those who receive it. That's the way God works in our lives and it is a great model for how we can work in the lives of others.

So let me ask you, what grade would you receive in Compassion Giving on your report card? I hope it's a good one, but I want to encourage you that there's always room for improvement for each of us. If you haven't been very good at Compassion Giving in the past, resolve to do better from this day forward. Listen to Mother Teresa's words one more time: "Yesterday is gone. Tomorrow has not yet come. We have only today. Let us begin."

That's good advice. Let's begin to be better Compassion Givers. Those who receive will be better for it. We who give will be better for it. The world will certainly be a better place, and think about how good it will make God feel.

This was a prayer of Mother Teresa: *Make us worthy, Lord, to serve the people throughout the world who live and die in poverty and hunger. Give them through our hands, this day, their daily bread, and by our understanding love, give them peace and joy.*

Notes:

A Prayer for Your Day

Heavenly Father, make us aware of the needs that sur-round us, and create in our hearts the desire to respond to these needs like You would. Help us to understand that not all poverty and hunger is on the other side of the world, and neither is it always something physical. Use us to bring Your compassion to those who need it. Every day. Change us in this process, make us more like You, until we respond in compassion to others like You do to us. Amen.

🌿

REFLECT & RESPOND

On a scale of 1 (callous) to 10 (compassionate), where do you rate yourself and why?

What two or three things can you do to move more toward the compassionate end of the scale?

How do you think others would rate you on the compassion scale, and on what basis do you think they would come to that judgment?

Compassion is possible because we are aware of and sensitive to the needs of others. How aware and sensitive are you? Ask God to help you become more aware, sensitive, and compassionate.

CHAPTER TWENTY

Thanks Giving

You can't get water from a dry sponge, and gratitude
won't flow from a hardened heart.

❧

*Then Jesus told him this story: "A man loaned money to
two people—five hundred pieces of silver to one and fifty
pieces to the other. But neither of them could repay him,
so he kindly forgave them both, canceling their debts.
Who do you suppose loved him more after that?"*
—LUKE 7:41-42 (NLT)

This is the last of five chapters on various types of giving and it's
also one that is different from the others in one very important
way. Generally speaking, the other chapters involve the what,
how, or when to give. Thanks Giving is about the why. Thanks
Giving is about the response, it's about the kind of giving that
gratitude produces. Thanks Giving only comes when we understand that each of us has received far more than we could ever
give. Without the gratitude that creates true Thanks Giving, the
other ways we give will ultimately become brittle rituals that satisfy neither us nor God. Thanks Giving is the oil that lubricates
the good steward's life and actions.

As we begin our conversation on Thanks Giving, I'd like to rephrase a proverb from the subject of wisdom to the subject of giving. *The Message* translates the need to get wisdom in these

> **Thanks Giving is a reflection of our hearts.**
> ❧

words: "Above all and before all, do this: Get Wisdom! Write this at the top of your list: Get Understanding!" (Proverbs 4:7). Changing the focus to giving with a few words, it would read: "Above all and before all, do this: Give Thankfully! Write this at the top of your list: Give Thankfully!" The reason why it is so important to have Thanks Giving as a top priority is because it is a reflection of our hearts; it sustains our stewardship in basic giving, helps us willingly make sacrifices, strengthens us in seasons of extraordinary commitment, and opens the doorway to the fulfillment of compassionately helping others. Thanks Giving is the engine that drives the train.

But Thanks Giving is not so much something that we strive to do as much as it is our response to what has been done for us. So the key that unlocks Thanks Giving in each of us begins with an accurate realization of who God is and who we are, and that begins with our acknowledgement that God is God and we're not. We are far less than God.

With very few exceptions most of the people I've met in my lifetime would agree that they're far from perfect, and this imperfection is a condition the Bible calls sin. Very unexpectedly, though, the perfect God decided to take our imperfections into

Notes:

His own hands and do something about them. *The Message* tells how Paul describes this: "God put the wrong on him who never did anything wrong, so we could be put right with God" (2 Corinthians 5:21). Please don't rush past this truth! If you've never heard it before or if you haven't yet experienced it, your heart isn't the place of gratitude that it could and should be. If you only know this as a hard-to-understand church doctrine or some other abstract thought, then your life isn't yet the one of peace, purpose, and joy that He intends for you.

This is important: if Thanks Giving is our *response* to something that has been done on our behalf, then it's not something that we can manufacture ourselves. We can't make ourselves be truly thankful any more than we can make ourselves be taller. But we can identify, understand, and embrace those things in our lives that will produce gratitude and Thanks Giving in us when they are given their proper recognition. Okay, what experiences have shaped an attitude of Thanks Giving in your life? We all have them, but sometimes we overlook how important they are. Let's take a look at some examples of how gratitude has been formed in others, and perhaps think of the ways it has shaped our lives. Imagine how you would respond if you or someone you loved was represented by one of these situations:

- In 1994, the Green family of California was having a wonderful vacation in Italy. But all that changed when seven-year-old Nicholas Green was shot and killed by robbers. Despite their personal grief, Nicholas' parents arranged to

Notes:

donate his organs, which went to seven transplant recipients. As news of the tragedy and the family's response spread around the world, many who heard the story became organ donors themselves in what became known as the Nicholas Effect. Imagine, though, if you were one of the seven who had been given a new lease on life. My guess is that these seven were changed by the magnitude of the sacrifice they received and by the gratitude in their hearts that followed, just as others are in similar circumstances.

• The book of Mark tells the story of a man named Jairus and his family. Jairus' daughter got sick and died before Jesus arrived to help. With Jesus, though, death didn't have the final say; He prayed and the girl's life returned. I love this story, but what really excites me is trying to put myself in the place of Jairus or his wife. What was it like for them, the parents of a child who had just been given back to them? I think musician Don Francisco described accurately their reaction in his ballad called "Gotta Tell Somebody." The song captures the response as the chorus excitedly repeats "Gotta tell somebody, gotta tell somebody, what Jesus did for me." Telling others about what happened wasn't an obligation for Jairus and his wife, it was an opportunity. That's the foundation of Thanks Giving.

• Fortunately for all of us, God is still in the business of returning the lives of sons and daughters to their parents.

Notes:

Several years ago I heard a woman speak about what it was like to see her son lost to drug addiction. At her emotional limit, frustrated and tired of failure, she could do no more to help. Then, when another crisis inevitably followed, Teen Challenge entered the picture. I remember hearing this mother, who once thought she had lost her son—and for the benefit of her own ability to cope emotionally, had started to act as if her son were no longer alive—proudly speak about the change and new life that took place through the ministry of Teen Challenge. Stop and think about how deep the gratitude must be in the heart of a mother who has regained her son. Thanks Giving is simply a natural expression in circumstances like these; Thanks Giving is the response of joy. If you've never heard a life-changing story like this, you're missing one of the great experiences of life.

• Imagine being wounded on a battlefield, surrounded by the sounds and fury of a deadly firefight. You're losing a battle to hold onto your life when, unbelievably, a medic or corpsman suddenly appears to bring medical care and comfort to you. Soon another miracle happens as a medevac pilot ignores the danger and lands his helicopter to evacuate you to the rear lines of safety and care. For many wounded veterans these aren't imaginations, they're memories. I know Army medics, Navy corpsmen, and helicopter pilots who served in Vietnam. Many men owe their lives to the work

Notes:

these brave heroes did, and many wouldn't have come home without these extraordinary efforts to save them. I wonder what the reunion of wounded and medic would be like, a reunion where the one whose life was saved had the opportunity to meet the one who made it possible. Wouldn't that be a place of gratitude and Thanks Giving? I think so.

The Bible reference at the top of this chapter is a story that Jesus used to illustrate an important principle. Let's read the rest of the story, beginning when Simon answers Jesus' question about who would love more:

"I suppose the one who had the bigger debt canceled." "You have judged correctly," Jesus said.

Then he turned toward the woman and said to Simon, "Do you see this woman? I came into your house. You did not give me any water for my feet, but she wet my feet with her tears and wiped them with her hair. You did not give me a kiss, but this woman, from the time I entered, has not stopped kissing my feet. You did not put oil on my head, but she has poured perfume on my feet. Therefore, I tell you, her many sins have been forgiven—for she loved much. But he who has been forgiven little loves little." (Luke 7:43-47)

Jesus is connecting our awareness of how much we have been forgiven to our ability to respond in love and gratitude to the One who has made this forgiveness possible. That makes sense to me,

Notes:

does it to you? After all, if we don't have a sense that something extraordinary has happened to us, what reason would there be for us to feel any sense of appreciation or gratitude? I've mentioned Teen Challenge several times, so far only as an organization, but one of the reasons Teen Challenge is so special is because of its people. They dedicate their lives to making it work. In many cases the staff members at a Teen Challenge facility have themselves been rescued from alcohol or drug abuse at one time by the work of Teen Challenge. I've had the privilege of hearing virtually the same story from literally hundreds of people helped by Teen Challenge: Life was out of control and to the point where it was not worth living. Thoughts or attempts of suicide were common. Loss of material possessions, relationships, and self-respect are a central part of each life story. These men and women tried drug therapy programs but they failed to bring any lasting change or hope for a future. Then God entered the picture through Teen Challenge and they finally realized they could be spiritually *forgiven* as well as physically rehabilitated. That forgiveness was and is life-changing. Graduates of Teen Challenge and their families are so grateful for what Teen Challenge has done for them that Thanks Giving is a natural result. If you visit a Teen Challenge center and talk with the staff, you'll see what I mean.

Thanksgiving 1968 was my last full day in Vietnam. I remember spending most of the day outside sitting on a sandbagged bunker, watching jetliners known as Freedom Birds land and take off at the huge Bien Hoa Air Base. The mess hall served the

Notes:

traditional Thanksgiving meal that day but I chose not to eat because the next day one of those Freedom Birds would be for me. After a fourteen-month absence I would finally be headed home to San Diego. That year my Thanksgiving dinner was a few days late but when it was finally served—a crisp quesadilla, tacos, enchiladas, and strawberry shortcake for dessert—I was a more thankful person than I'd ever been before. Two years later I got married and my wife Pam taught me even deeper understandings of what it means to be a grateful person, one for whom Thanks Giving is a natural response. Being loved much changes a person much and it makes them more loving and grateful in return.

Those on a Steward's Journey never reach a final destination where God's love and forgiveness are perfectly understood. I'm glad for this. The prophet Jeremiah wrote this wonderful promise: "His mercies begin afresh each day" (Lamentations 3:23, NLT). And they do. Every morning the good steward wakes to discover new gifts from God and every day he welcomes those gifts with Thanks Giving. Good stewards have grateful attitudes that attract, smiles that encourage, actions that demonstrate care and compassion. By their generous giving of time, talent, and treasure they reflect the generosity that has been *lavished* (Ephesians 1:8) on them. Are these qualities that reflect your life today? They can be! Thanks Giving is possible for each of us because those who have been forgiven much—that means all of us—love much.

Notes:

A Prayer for Your Day

Heavenly Father, help us to be truly thankful people because we understand how much You have done for us. Keep us sensitive to You, keep us close to You, keep us centered in You. Help us never to get far from an aware-ness of Your love and forgiveness. Make Thanks Giving a natural part of our lives. Make it something that flows from us and not something manufactured on our own. Thank You that this is Your way and a better way. Amen.

❧

REFLECT & RESPOND

Reflect on how the following sentence describes your personal experience: "Without the gratitude that creates true Thanks Giving, the other ways we give will ultimately become brittle rituals that satisfy neither us nor God."

Ask God to show you how much He has done for you, and make a comprehensive list of things that you can be grateful for. Then reflect on whether your life demonstrates appropriate Thanks Giving.

Is there anything in your life that means so much to you that it makes you "Gotta Tell Somebody"? Do you? In what ways?

CHAPTER TWENTY-ONE

Inspiration Point

It's amazing how many times extraordinary things happen to ordinary people when they seek God's vision and values.

🌿

God saw all that he had made, and it was very good.
—GENESIS 1:31

If you live long enough and are fortunate enough to travel, you're blessed to see the beauty that God has built into the earth. I qualify on both accounts, years and miles, and I have to say that God does really good work. It's hard to imagine anything more majestic than the Yosemite Valley in the morning, or more spectacular than the painted skies of a Hawaiian sunset. To see them is to be inspired at how very good His creation is. Yet even more awesome and inspiring is the work He accomplishes in a human life. Today we're going to pause our journey as we did in chapter 9, pull over at one of the many inspirational points along the way, and look at what He's done.

Pastor Dan Betzer has a heart to share the Good News with those who've never heard. Today, he is the pastor of a large and thriving congregation on Florida's west coast. But it wasn't always so. The following is a summary of his story, taken from a message he gave to fellow ministers.

A once sizable congregation had dwindled to about 400, and those that remained were saddled with an unmanageable multi-million dollar debt. The church was in default on its loans, one for $100,000 and the other for $2 million, and was seriously at risk of losing its property. In the midst of this situation Pastor Betzer felt strongly that God was calling his church to make a significant financial commitment to missions, and he scheduled a Missions Convention where members of the congregation committed more than $223,000.

Shortly thereafter, with the crisis growing, Pastor Betzer received a phone call from a man he'd not previously met. Could they have lunch? Sure. The man explained that he'd first attended the church at the Missions Convention meetings and he shared his concern over the church's poor financial health. Then he took out a checkbook and handed a $100,000 check to his new pastor. But that wasn't all. He explained to Pastor Betzer that while he wasn't in a position to give the $2 million needed to resolve the second loan, he could loan it to the church. *That afternoon.* It's a great story, but how did it happen? I think Pastor Betzer would explain that if churches, or people, aren't doing those things that are important to God, there's no reason for God to answer their prayers for help. God is in the redemption business, and when His people join Him

Notes:

in His business, there's no limit to what can be done. When churches and people make a serious investment in giving to those things that are close to God's heart, they open themselves to blessings that would never have been experienced otherwise.[1]

Remember the subject of chapter 9, when God gives His vision, He also gives His provision? That's what happened here. When Pastor Betzer's church embraced the vision to fund missionary efforts, it embraced God's vision, and as we've seen elsewhere, God's provision flows to those people and places that share His vision.

> It's amazing how many times extra-ordinary things happen to ordinary people when they seek to share God's vision and values.
>
> ❧

Admittedly, the unexpected gift of $100,000 and the instant provision of a $2 million loan are extraordinary events. But it's amazing how many times extraordinary things happen to ordinary people when they seek to share God's vision and values. I'd like to share five more instances of God working to and through His people. I'm changing the names of the people involved to maintain the focus on what God did, and not on those who benefited by His acts.

- Barbara had not been married long when she was abandoned by her husband for another woman. I can't pretend to know how scary it was for her to suddenly find herself divorced, alone, and in immediate need to earn a living. Yet

---

Notes:

in the midst of this personal crisis, Barbara's faith held fast. As she considered her financial condition and prepared a meager budget, she felt strongly that she should make a generous annual commitment to support various missions projects. Acting in faith, she committed to give the equivalent of one month's salary for this purpose every year, even though when she did, she sensed she was sacrificing two things that she valued: travel and the ability to have a new car every four or five years. I can still remember when Barbara shared about what God did for her: "For eight years I waited to see what God would do, and watched Him provide in special ways for me every year, without fail." One year her washer and dryer broke down and she was given free replacements. One year her boss had a schedule change and couldn't take a long-planned trip to Italy! He offered Barbara the opportunity to go in his place. She was given a company car. She was the only one in her position to be offered stock options. Every year it was something different, and each year it was faith-building. Barbara didn't make a giving commitment in order to get anything from God. She made her commitment in obedience to what she sensed He wanted her to do. Yet somewhere on her stewardship journey, her sacrifices became her blessings.

• One evening, in the midst of her own personal crisis that was very similar to Barbara's circumstances, Christine heard Barbara share her story of God's faithfulness. Christine

---

Notes:

thought to herself, *If God was faithful to Barbara, maybe I can trust Him too.* Christine sought God's direction for how she should respond and she eventually made a financial commitment to help extend the influence of her local church in the community. Nearly a year later, I began hearing wonderful things about Christine and what God was doing in her life. I called to see if she would share her story with the church congregation and was startled to hear her respond, "No." She went on to explain, "I would have only three or four minutes to share with the congregation, but it would take me at least twenty or thirty minutes to describe how God has blessed me." Wouldn't you like to have a story about God's blessing that you couldn't tell in just three or four minutes? You would be a living example of what Paul wrote about in Ephesians 3:20: "God can do anything, you know—far more than you could ever imagine or guess or request in your wildest dreams" (MSG). What He did for Barbara and He did for Christine, He can do for any of us.

- I love this story about Tim and Beth, but I need to preface it with a brief explanation, because it's my experience that no matter what the sign on the clothing rack says, one size never fits all. In chapter 18 we talked about Extraordinary Giving and in the next chapter we're going to talk about A Steward's Guide to Giving. Extraordinary Giving is extraordinarily personal. It involves seeking direction and then responding obediently once the direction is given. What

Notes:

God called Tim and Beth to do is not for everyone. But I'm glad it was for them and I'm glad we have their story.

Tim was the pastor of a church that had outgrown its space and needed to build a new sanctuary. At the same time, Tim and Beth had listed their home for sale and were planning to move to a larger house for their growing family. As Tim wrestled with how his family could respond in a sacrificial way, he sensed that God was prompting him to sell their house, but then give the equity to the church building project. They would rent until they could afford to buy another home. Now I don't know about you, but if I received that direction it wouldn't be the easiest subject to bring up with my wife. But Tim did, and Beth agreed. At an appropriate occasion, Tim shared the decision with his congregation. Here's where it gets really interesting. Tim and Beth were completely unaware that another couple in their church was on a Steward's Journey of their own, and that the two journeys were about to intersect. For the couple in the congregation who sat listening to Tim and Beth's story, it was an answer to a year-long prayer. They went home, talked things through, prayed, and that evening asked for a meeting with Tim. "We want to make the down payment on your new house," they said, and then went on to explain. For almost a year this couple had a substantial amount of money set aside to give to God's work, but they didn't know where it should go. Their repeated prayers for

Notes:

guidance were always answered with the same sense of direction: "Wait, I have something special I want to do with that money." Something special, indeed. Tim and Beth's willingness to obey God in the extraordinarily difficult decision they made, became the long-awaited answer to a generous couple's prayer. Just as important, when the congregation saw how the sacrificial gift of their pastor became the answer to prayer for another couple, the result was a huge breakthrough in giving. The entire congregation gained a new sense for what God could and would do through their combined efforts. Not only was the new sanctuary built, but just as importantly, the people of the church had their faith strengthened as they responded to their responsibilities as stewards.

• Speaking of pastors, houses, and sacrifices, one Saturday morning I sat across the breakfast table from a pastor and his wife, anxious to hear what was happening in their church. Before we started that conversation, though, the pastor took the conversation in a different direction. He wanted to tell me about their new house. Like Tim and Beth, the pastor and his wife had decided about a year previously to delay the purchase of a new home. Instead, they chose to make a significant gift to help their church hire a youth pastor and reach more young people in the surrounding community. The financial commitment they made to expand the ministry of their church was approximately

Notes:

what would have been required for a down payment on a home. It hadn't been an easy decision. But the pastor shared with me how God had then provided a down payment for a new home from a completely unexpected source. What a blessing it was for me to listen as these two faithful stewards told me all about their new house—in words and smiles.

• My last story is one that I've heard repeated many times; it's a story shared by men and women, young and old. For some of you it might not appear very spectacular, but if you've been in the room when the story was told you'd know why the story never grows old for me. It's a story of God's simple response to obedience and it usually follows this pattern. A person is challenged to make a financial commitment and responds—with absolutely no idea of how it can be fulfilled. Then, within days or weeks, something happens. A promotion. A retroactive raise and back pay, for as much as a year! An unexpected check in the mail. A phone notification of a forgotten bank account. The details are different but the essence is always the same: God's provision. He wants to work in His people and through His people to let others know about Him. One evening in central California, I was in a meeting where three people shared virtually the same story! Just a few weeks before they'd made a financial commitment to become more generous people. Within days, and in one instance early the next morning, each person experienced miraculous provi-

Notes:

sion. They experienced enough provision to fulfill their financial commitments, and they received more than enough provision to strengthen their faith.

If all this seems new to you, that's okay. For the people in this chapter, every story represented a time when God did something new in their lives. As you continue a Steward's Journey, my prayer is that you will experience something new and know the tremendous joy and satisfaction that comes with generosity.

A Prayer for Your Day

Heavenly Father, bring me to the place on my journey where I experience provision that can only be explained as coming from You. Use this time to build my faith in Your faithfulness. Use it to encourage others and to cause them to trust You more. Just like Barbara's story inspired Christine, let my story influence someone who needs to know how much You care for them and for the world. Amen.

❧

REFLECT & RESPOND

Have you ever experienced God's provision in an inspiring way like those in this chapter did and, if so, how did it change you?

Have you ever known someone or been present when someone shared a story like those in this chapter and, if so, how did it make you feel?

Ask God to show you, in a very personal way, how sufficient His provision is to meet your needs.

Consider reading about the lives of faithful stewards in the past, so that you can see how God is able to inspire and meet the needs of His people. Ask your pastor or the manager of a Christian bookstore to suggest some appropriate book titles.

CHAPTER TWENTY-TWO

A Steward's Guide to Giving

Read. Pray. Listen. Obey.

❦

If you need wisdom—if you want to know what
God wants you to do—ask him, and he will
gladly tell you. He will not resent your asking.

—JAMES 1:5, NLT

There was a time, seemingly a lifetime ago, when I voluntarily jumped out of what my friends described as "perfectly good airplanes." With several hundred others, I was assigned to a class at the U.S. Army Jump School in Fort Benning, Georgia. We learned all about parachutes and how to land without breaking a leg, a neck, or worse. Then it was time for practice, lots of practice. We started on a step just 18 inches off the ground, then graduated to a 34-foot tower, and finally we were hoisted by cable to the top of a 250-foot tower—then dropped. We did just about everything short of actually jumping through an open door at 1200 feet. But each of us knew that practice wasn't enough. We knew that if we were going to be paratroopers, we had to jump.

Being a true steward is not too different. There's a time for learning and a time for doing. It's important to read and learn about the theory of stewardship, but knowledge and understanding aren't enough. There comes a point in every Steward's Journey when stewardship moves from the realm of the theoretical to the practical. So let's talk about a practical guide to giving.

Some might prefer a quick and easy guide to deciding how much to give to various causes, because it seems that we're constantly faced with requests or opportunities to give. Wouldn't it be nice to have a built-in stewardship formula included in Microsoft Excel? Or perhaps a *Dummies Quick Reference Giving Guide?* They might be easier, but I don't think the pattern of Scripture points us to unthinking formulas. There are some basic principles, however, that can help us arrive at our everyday giving decisions. Most of these have already been suggested, but let's see if we can use them to build a set of useful guidelines.

BE WILLING

The first step in our guidelines to giving is to be open and willing to do so. We've already seen in earlier chapters how important it is that our gifts are made willingly, and not reluctantly. Even after four centuries of slavery, ancient Israel gave willingly to build a tabernacle in the wilderness (Exodus 35–36). King David and his leaders gave willingly to provide materials to build a temple (1 Chronicles 29). And, of course, Jesus did not hold on

Notes:

to His divine rights, instead choosing to give Himself willingly to bridge the separation between mankind and God (Philippians 2). In churches where I've taught about stewardship I've asked this question: "Would you be willing to pray about being willing to give?" That's the best starting point for all of us: simply being willing. In fact, I think this is such an important factor that, in the life of mature stewards, they eventually stop asking how much do they *have* to give and begin to ask how much *can* they give.

READ GOD'S WORD

The Bible is unique among all the books that have ever been written, because it claims to be more than words written on parchment or printed on paper. The Bible claims to be a living word with the ability to powerfully impact lives in ways no mere book could do. Consider this reference from the book of Hebrews: "For the word of God is living and active" (4:12). *The Message* translates the remainder of the passage this way: "His powerful Word is sharp as a surgeon's scalpel, cutting through everything, whether doubt or defense, laying us open to listen and obey. Nothing and no one is impervious to God's Word. We can't get away from it— no matter what" (4:12-13).

What a powerful statement! The Bible claims for itself the unique ability to influence and change lives, and the evidence that supports its claim is all around us. Consider this scenario:

Notes:

A man checks into a hotel. The circumstances of his life are so overwhelmingly negative that the will to live is gone. He checked in to the hotel to check out of life. Minutes away from suicide, he opens a bureau drawer, finds a Bible, and opens it. Something catches his eye, and as he reads, everything changes. For the first time in a long time, it's as if he can breathe again. Death is no longer an option; it's replaced by a newfound drive to live.

This scenario is not fictional. It happens, more often than we can imagine. I've been in meetings where people shared this hypothetical scenario as their personal story. They were changed in a moment, when a printed word on a page became a living Word in their lives.

Another passage of the Bible explains this: "In the beginning was the Word, and the Word was with God, and the Word was God. He was with God in the beginning" (John 1:1). *The Message* continues later in the passage with this translation: "The Word became flesh and blood, and moved into the neighborhood. We saw the glory with our own eyes, the one-of-a-kind glory, like Father, like Son, Generous inside and out, true from start to finish " (John 1:14).

I really don't want to get too theological here, but it's important to say that when we read the Bible for guidance on giving and stewardship matters, we approach more than words—we approach The Word. We approach God Himself, the original source of generosity. This is absolutely beyond our comprehension, but it's an awesome thought for us to consider.

Notes:

PRAY

I can't tell you how many times I've heard that there's no such thing as a bad question. If that's true, why have I seen so many facial expressions that strongly suggested that I have asked one during a conversation? Know the feeling? If so, I have good news.

Take another look at the verse at the start of this chapter. It says, "If you need wisdom—if you want to know what God wants you to do—ask him, and he will gladly tell you. He will not resent your asking" (NLT).

Think about the fact that if we need wisdom, we can ask what God wants us to do without being afraid that we've just asked a bad question. He does not resent our asking! Not only that, but He will gladly tell us what He wants us to do. These aren't just my words, shared with you over a cup of coffee. These are, as we just saw in the previous section, *living words*. This is God's Word, and it will give us wisdom as we build guidelines for giving.

Let's look at another verse: "And we can be confident that he will listen to us whenever we ask him for anything in line with his will. And if we know he is listening when we make our requests, we can be sure that he will give us what we ask for" (1 John 5:14-16, NLT).

Prayer is absolutely essential when it comes to our knowing *what* we should give, *when,* and *to whom.* If we need wisdom, ask. If we ask, He hears us. If He hears us, we can confidently expect his personal answer for us.

So, how do we go about praying for guidance in giving? First,

Notes:

make sure you understand why you're being asked to give. What's the vision that is driving the request? Is it close to God's heart? Or motivated by something less honorable? Second, be open to what God wants to give through you. Remember what we talked about in chapters 9 and 11. Maybe God wants this process to result in more than a monetary gift; maybe He wants to reveal something about the scope of His character and His resources to you. Being open to God's will means breaking down artificial limits that we often impose on ourselves. Third, give yourself time. The verses in this section promise an answer, but they don't promise it instantly. Some things shouldn't be rushed, and prayer is one.

"Dear God, I want to know Your will and I need to know Your mind. I accept the confidence that You have promised, I trust that You will give the wisdom I need, so give me insight is my prayer. How do You see this matter, God? Show me Your heart for it. Make clear what You want me to do. Help me understand how I make a difference. I'm waiting for Your answer. Amen."

LISTEN

Listening is an important but often neglected part of virtually every relationship. Prayer is no exception.

There is a difference between listening *to* something and listening *for* something. Here's an illustration of the difference.

Most of us are in our cars every day, many times with the radio on. But I know, at least in my case, that I'm not really paying close

Notes:

attention. It's just background noise. I'm listening *to* something on the radio. But suppose I knew that the radio station had a contest—with a grand prize that I'd really like to win? It involved the radio personality occasionally reading a name on air, maybe even my name. To win, all I needed to do was call the station when I heard my name called. If I really want to hear my name, my level of attention would definitely increase. Now I'm no longer listening *to* something, I'm listening *for* something.

The answer to prayer doesn't always come with a loud knock on the door. The Old Testament prophet Elijah heard it in "the sound of a gentle whisper" (1 Kings 19:12, NLT). Let me point out the obvious: it's hard to hear a whisper when we're surrounded by shouting voices.

> **It's hard to hear a whisper when we're surrounded by shouting voices.**
> ❧

Here's another promise for us from Scripture: "After he has gathered his own flock, he walks ahead of them, and they follow him because they recognize his voice. They won't follow a stranger; they will run from him because they don't recognize his voice" (John 10:4-5, NLT). Many times I have heard people express this concern: "How will I know the answer, and how will I know that it's from God?" Because if your heart is willing, and you're looking for truth in His Word, and you have prayed for His direction, He promises to answer, and He promises that you will recognize His voice. Remember, our prayers aren't over until we've listened *for* the answer. And received it.

Notes:

OBEY

Just as King Saul learned in a conversation with Samuel, obedience might be the hardest part of all. "But Samuel replied, 'What is more pleasing to the LORD: your burnt offerings or your obedience to his voice? Obedience is far better than sacrifice'" (1 Samuel 15:22, NLT). Saul thought that because he gave a substantial offering to the Lord, he would be excused for not giving what the Lord had told him. When we have been in the place of prayer and heard His voice, we are expected to obey it. Even if what we hear takes us out of our comfort zones. Carol Cymbala said it perfectly in her book *He's Been Faithful:* "If you really want God to use you, then you have to be willing to follow him into uncomfortable places and to do things you simply can't do on a natural level."[1] She's right!

Here's something maybe you haven't considered that I'd like you to think about. I believe that in every area of our lives God is looking for ways to reveal more of Himself and His purposes to us. That includes how we exercise stewardship and arrive at our giving decisions. That leads to a question: If we remain in our comfort zone, how can we learn anything new about God or His purpose for us? If we decide to give an amount that is totally within our ability to give, where is the opportunity for our faith to grow? If, on the other hand, we depend on His unexpected and extraordinary provision to meet the commitment, our faith will be strengthened when He acts on our behalf, and our willingness

---

Notes:

to believe for even greater provision in the future will be increased. But all of this requires obedience.

It wasn't easy for David to challenge Goliath. Or Peter and John to grasp the hand of a cripple and pull him to his feet. ("But God, if You don't show up, he'll collapse and we'll look bad!") Or ancient Israel to surround the heavily fortified city of Jericho. It wasn't easy, but it was obedient. Imagine, though, how faith was increased in each of these cases when God was released to act on behalf of His people.

Another way of saying that we are called to obey is to remind ourselves that we are people who are called to actions that are consistent with our confessed beliefs. James says it this way in *The Message:* "Don't fool yourself into thinking that you are a listener when you are anything but, letting the Word go in one ear and out the other. Act on what you hear!" (James 1:22).

Obedience isn't easy, but obedience opens the doors of blessing. When you reach out your hand to open the door, understand that He promises to be with you, just as He told ancient Israel four times in the first chapter of Joshua. *Be strong and courageous* was His word then and it His word for us now.

CONFIRMATION

Okay, our guidelines say to be willing, read, pray, listen, and obey. But is there any way to confirm that we've arrived at the amount and the place God really intended for us to give? Paul shares two

---

Notes:

examples in 2 Corinthians 8 that I think can be helpful in confirming what He wants us to do.

With God, it's possible to give more than we can afford. That's the conclusion from the example of the first century Macedonian church: "Fierce troubles came down on the people of those churches, pushing them to the very limit. The trial exposed their true colors: They were incredibly happy, though desperately poor. The pressure triggered something totally unexpected: an outpouring of pure and generous gifts. I was there and saw it for myself. They gave offerings of whatever they could—far more than they could afford!" (2 Corinthians 8:2-3, MSG). I believe those who don't think they can do more, or tend to always remain in their comfort zones, should consider the fact that the Macedonians gave more than they could afford. In purely human terms that doesn't make sense. It shouldn't be possible to give more than we are able to give. The steward, though, has more resources to draw upon than just his own. So, the first confirmation question is this: *Am I trusting God and responding to what I've heard from Him, even if I don't understand how it can happen?* Maybe you've heard the expression that God comforts the afflicted and afflicts the comforted. This first question is for the *comforted,* who perhaps need to be *afflicted* to believe God for more.

There's another group, though, that tends to always wish to do more. For this group, it's easy to suffer from self-condemnation because they can't do all they'd like to do. I see this group as the *afflicted* class, in need of *comfort.* God has a word for them, too. Just

---

Notes:

a few sentences after Paul wrote about the Macedonian example, he gave us this promise: "For if the willingness is there, the gift is acceptable according to what one has, not according to what he does not have" (2 Corinthians 8:12). The question for this group is: *Does my heart genuinely desire to give more?* If so, Paul says that the gift is acceptable, regardless of the amount. There's no conflict here, only a divine recognition that some of us tend toward safety and need to be challenged to respond in faith, while others tend toward self-condemnation, and need to rest in His acceptance. There are no formulas; no one can tell another which category they're in. Except God. Listen to Him and you'll be just fine.

A Prayer for Your Day

Heavenly Father, You have promised to give wisdom to those who ask You for it, and I am asking now. Show me in Your Word what it is that You want me to do about my giving. Cause me to want to seek Your counsel and speak with You in prayer. Let me hear Your voice clearly, and give me the courage to respond in obedience to Your direction. In this entire process may I discover more about who You are. Thank You that I can be confident that asking for Your wisdom is something that You want me to do, and is a prayer that You delight in answering. Amen.

❧

REFLECT & RESPOND

Review Scripture references in the chapters you've completed already on *A Steward's Journey* and ask God to reveal those passages He wants you to meditate about now.

Pray about how God specifically wants you to respond to giving circumstances that are facing you at this time.

Resolve to be patient and continue seeking God until you hear His answer for you.

Reflect on this reference: "Obedience is far better than sacrifice" (1 Samuel 15:22, MSG). Ask God to help you obey His direction.

CHAPTER TWENTY-THREE

A Steward's Guide to Living

Tomorrow is not guaranteed. Take care of today.

✹

*Look here, you people who say, "Today or tomorrow we are
going to a certain town and will stay there a year.
We will do business there and make a profit."
How do you know what will happen tomorrow?*
—JAMES 4:13-14, NLT

In 1976 Francis Schaeffer wrote an important book titled *How
Should We Then Live?*[1] Schaeffer was a brilliant thinker and I
remember struggling to understand his thoughts about how
people of faith should live in a culture that was moving away from
acknowledging God's existence. The question Schaeffer asked in
his book title is certainly a valid one for us to consider today. How
should a steward live? What is our guide for living? How can we
make that guide more understandable and practical enough to
help us in our daily decision-making? Let's talk about that today.

Schaeffer described a culture that was increasingly at odds with
biblical teaching, and that's the reality faced by stewards every day.

In the reference in the beginning of this chapter, James talked about those who make plans without factoring God into the equation, without considering that there's more to life than what they can plan. *The Message* captures this distinction in its translation.

> And now I have a word for you who brashly announce, "Today—at the latest, tomorrow—we're off to such and such a city for the year. We're going to start a business and make a lot of money." You don't know the first thing about tomorrow. You're nothing but a wisp of fog, catching a brief bit of sun before disappearing. Instead, make it a habit to say, "If the Master wills it and we're still alive, we'll do this or that." (James 4:13-15)

Ours is increasingly a culture of self. It's all about being self-made, self-sufficient, self-actualized. I think Scripture would describe this behavior as self-ish.

The error James pointed out was not that people made plans for the future but that they didn't include God in their plans. That's not a mistake the steward can afford because good stewards center their very existence on the reality of God at work in their lives. Going one step further, good stewards look to maximize each moment, each opportunity, each interaction. Stewards understand the importance of the present, partly because it's what good stewardship demands, but also because we can only be assured of what is facing us *now;* tomorrow isn't guaranteed.

Stewards take care of today and Paul advises us on how:

Notes:

So here's what I want you to do, God helping you: Take your everyday, ordinary life—your sleeping, eating, going-to-work, and walking-around life—and place it before God as an offering. Embracing what God does for you is the best thing you can do for him. Don't become so well-adjusted to your culture that you fit into it without even thinking. Instead, fix your attention on God. You'll be changed from the inside out. Readily recognize what he wants from you, and quickly respond to it. Unlike the culture around you, always dragging you down to its level of immaturity, God brings the best out of you, develops well-formed maturity in you. (Romans 12:1-2, MSG)

There's a lot to think about in that paragraph so let's break it down into eight points to form our Steward's Guide to Living.

1. *God helping you.* Stewards begin by acknowledging that they can't succeed without God's help. This is a very simple concept that is too often overlooked.

2. *Take your everyday, ordinary life.* Stewards don't dedicate a portion of themselves, some super-spiritual religious component of their lives, to God. No, stewards dedicate the routine of their daily lives to God, and that means all the carpools, business trips, housekeeping, meal preparation, leisure, schoolwork, and so on. It means *everything!* It means that stewards live generously even in the routine parts of their lives. Thanks Giving? Stewards live the routine of their lives thankfully.

Notes:

Stewards live sacrificially. Stewards live contentedly. Stewards live within their means. Stewards live compassionately. Stewards make right choices. They don't just reserve these characteristics for the "religious" part of their lives; they live them out in everything.

3. *Embracing what God does for you.* Embracing God's work in us goes far beyond merely acknowledging it. If you meet a friend or relative at the airport, someone you haven't seen for a long time, you can acknowledge them when you see them with a wave of the hand or you can embrace them. There's a big difference. Stewards throw their arms around what God is doing in their lives and they welcome His work. Paul says the steward can bring no better offering to God than this.

4. *Don't become so well-adjusted to your culture that you fit into it without even thinking.* Stewards are aware of what is happening around them. They aren't tricked into believing in something that isn't true because they base their lives and existence on what is true. They know the difference, and they understand the damage that comes from following the culture without thinking—without testing it against the counsel of Scripture. They're guided by reading what God says and praying for His direction. They don't listen to the counsel of the culture because they value listening to how

> Stewards fix themselves on the things of God and the things of God become fixed in them.
> 🍃

Notes:

God answers their prayers even more. And stewards have the courage to obey, even when they seem to be the only ones living the way they do.

5. *Fix your attention on God.* Stewards focus on God because He is their source, their resource, their reality, their example. Focus brings change. We become more like Him.

6. *You'll be changed from the inside out.* This is really important. We can't change ourselves from the outside in, but He can change us from the inside out. Stewards fix themselves on the things of God and the things of God become fixed in them. Stewardship isn't like putting on a suit of clothes so that we'll be appropriately dressed for the occasion; stewardship is a matter of the heart that makes us prepared for any occasion.

7. *Readily recognize what He wants from you, and quickly respond to it.* There's no way for us to know what God wants from us if we aren't in a close and constant relationship with Him. It's just not possible. If we aren't reading, praying, and listening we won't know what we're supposed to do. But it doesn't stop there—stewards *respond.* That takes obedience and obedience is a chief characteristic of every good steward. Responding isn't always easy but it's always right.

8. *God brings out the best in you.* For many years the army recruiting slogan was "Be All That You Can Be." I have to confess that my army experience made me better, but the best? No, that takes God. And that brings stewards to an

Notes:

exciting new awareness of what can happen to and through them as God works in their lives. Stewards don't settle for better, they know they can be the best.

We're almost done for today, but here are a few final thoughts.

- Stewards are masters of the moment. They're not looking for fulfillment tomorrow, they're discovering it today. Master your moments.

- Stewards order priorities. They understand what's important and they keep the main thing the main thing. They keep their possessions in perspective.

- Stewards live generously yet graciously. They understand that all they have to give, money and otherwise, is only a small return on what God has given to them. The result is a humble spirit that honors God.

- Stewards leave legacies. Proverbs 13:22 says, "A good man leaves an inheritance for his children's children." This is a wonderful promise. Notice the verse says nothing about the *rich* man leaving an inheritance, it speaks about the *good* man. Regardless of the size of our estate, if we've been good stewards we will leave an inheritance. Notice also that the inheritance extends not just to our children, a single generation, but to our children's children. It probably takes a grandpa or grandma to fully appreciate the treasure in that promise.

How should we then live? I think that living as good stewards makes a great answer to that question. Do you agree?

Notes:

A Prayer for Your Day

Heavenly Father, teach us how to live in a culture that tries to ignore You. Teach us so well that the culture will not be able to ignore the example of our lives. Teach us everything we need to know by teaching us about You. Help us to fix ourselves on You so that You can change us from the inside out. Make us our best. Make our lives a legacy for others in future generations. Only You can do this. Only in You do we trust. Amen.

❦

REFLECT & RESPOND

How do you invite God to help you in everyday living?

How much do you *embrace* those things that God is doing in your life?

Have you become too well-adjusted to the message of our culture?

How do you fix your attention on God whenever possible?

How easy is it for you to recognize what He wants you to do and for you to respond to His direction?

How often do you ask God to bring out the best in you and thank Him when He does?

CHAPTER TWENTY-FOUR

Who Gets the Credit?

True stewards don't give to get. They give to glorify.

❦

But who am I, and who are my people, that we should be
able to give as generously as this? Everything comes from you,
and we have given you only what comes from your hand.

—1 CHRONICLES 29:14

I'd like to paint you a word picture about Christmas morning. The traditional family breakfast is over, the dishes have been washed and put away, and the kitchen readied for the start of Christmas dinner. I don't know about in your house, but in ours we seem to drag this time out, hoping the excitement of gift-giving will last longer. Finally, though, the packages can't be ignored any longer and everyone settles into their usual place on the sofa, floor, or a favorite chair. The most excited person in the house usually volunteers to be Santa's helper and little stacks form as each person is given their gifts. A familiar scene? Probably. Let's focus on one specific gift, a gift of yours. What it is doesn't matter, it could be something for your home, workbench, wardrobe, or favorite hobby. What matters is that it's something you've always wanted. Nice picture? It's just perfect!

But suppose the picture didn't end on Christmas Day. Suppose there was another image titled "What If?" that followed a few days or weeks later. What if the person who gave you the gift was always nearby, watching, to let you know you weren't using their gift "correctly"? What if you weren't free to enjoy the gift because it was always subject to what the gift-giver thought? Worse, what if you were expected to respond to the gift by doing things that the gift-giver wanted you to do or risk their displeasure. What if the gift-giver let you know that there wouldn't be any more gifts if you weren't sufficiently appreciative? What if something like this happened to you? How would you feel? I think all my joy in the gift would evaporate when I discovered it came with conditions tied to it.

Unfortunately, sometimes gifts given to the church or worthwhile ministries are made with such strings attached. You see it in attitudes: "I should be able to choose the carpet color since I paid for it"; or "We should be consulted before any changes are made in the order of the Sunday morning service"; or "They can't sell those chairs, my parents bought them." Gifts made with such conditions are no gifts at all, they are down payments on a controlling interest in how the church or ministry is operated. Gifts with strings attached open the door to manipulation that can cripple the effectiveness of a church. Gifts with conditions are not about stewardship, they are about self-centeredness.

There are other ways we dishonor God even though on the outside it might appear that we are honoring Him with our gifts. One way is to brag about our giving and call attention to ourselves

Notes:

rather than to the generosity of a Creator who makes it possible. This strikes me as a type of spiritual plagiarism that takes credit for the work of another, and plagiarism is a form of stealing. It takes something away from its rightful owner. Stewards acknowledge God's hand, they don't emphasize their own.

Scripture talks about gifts that are given that aren't consistent with good stewardship. In chapter 13 we learned from the book of Isaiah that God is more interested in the heart of the giver than He is in the size of the gift (1:11-17). Throughout Scripture we see these recurring thoughts: True stewards don't give to get, they give to glorify because they understand their ability to give anything at all originated with God's equipping them to give. True stewards don't brag about what they give, they are humbled by their ability to give as they faithfully seek to manage what God has placed in their care. True stewards don't give with strings attached, they give in order to release blessings in the lives of others. True stewards know it's not about them.

Look at David's wonderful affirmation given at the start of this chapter, this time taken from *The Message*:

> But me—who am I, and who are these my people, that we
> should presume to be giving something to you? Everything
> comes from you; all we're doing is giving back what we've been
> given from your generous hand…. GOD, our God, all these
> materials—these piles of stuff for building a house of worship for
> you, honoring your Holy Name—it all came from you! It was all

---

Notes:

yours in the first place! I know, dear God, that you care nothing for the surface—you want us, our true selves—and so I have given from the heart, honestly and happily. And now see all these people doing the same, giving freely, willingly—what a joy! O GOD, God of our fathers Abraham, Isaac, and Israel, keep this generous spirit alive forever in these people always, keep their hearts set firmly in you. (1 Chronicles 29:14-18)

David didn't think the gifts he gave were something to boast about; how could they be when they came first from God? Isaiah said it this way: "For all we have accomplished is really from you" (26:12, NLT).

The good steward lives in the recognition that all that is accomplished is really from Him. Let's take another look at some of the primary scriptures in Section Two.

- "For who do you know that really knows you, knows your heart? And even if they did, is there anything they would discover in you that you could take credit for?" (1 Corinthians 4:7, MSG)
- "The earth is the LORD's, and everything in it, the world, and all who live in it." (Psalms 24:1)
- "Christ is the one through whom God created everything in heaven and earth…. Everything has been created through him and for him." (Colossians 1:16, NLT)

These verses don't leave much room for us to claim credit. The credit belongs to God.

There is, however, a time when we will be credited for our

Notes:

actions and our giving. Only instead of us claiming credit for our-selves, it will be God crediting us with faithful stewardship of His accounts. That's the lesson taught in the parable of the talents described in Matthew 25. That's the time when it will really mat-ter. Until then, let's give credit where credit is due, to the One who made us and gave us abilities we can use to give back to Him.

There's really not much more to be said. We understand from our own human experience that we don't like it when we receive gifts with strings attached, so why should God like it any more than we do? Our society discredits those who plagiarize the work of others and claim credit for themselves that they don't deserve. Why should God view this less seriously than our culture does? The answers, of course, are that He doesn't. The good steward knows this. Because it's not about the steward; it's about the stew-ard's Source. God gets the credit.

A Prayer for Your Day

Heavenly Father, help each of us to give You the credit You deserve. Keep us from reserving any credit for ourselves. We agree today with David's prayer to "keep this generous spirit alive forever in us, keep our hearts set firmly in You." Teach us to give generously with no conditions. Teach us the joy that is found in doing this. Teach us the heart attitude of the good steward. Amen.

❦

REFLECT & RESPOND

How do you feel when someone takes credit they don't deserve?

Do you respond positively or negatively when you hear that someone has plagiarized the work of another? How would you feel if it were your work that was stolen?

Describe your reaction when you are around those who properly deflect credit away from themselves and toward those who rightfully deserve it?

When you are involved in success how do you express your thanks to Him for making it all possible?

CHAPTER TWENTY-FIVE

The Multiplication Factor

There's no limit to what can be accomplished
when we are willing to let God be God.

❧

*Remember this—a farmer who plants only a few seeds will get a small
crop. But the one who plants generously will get a generous crop.
You must each make up your own mind how much you should give.*
—2 CORINTHIANS 9:6-7, NLT

Can you remember what it was like when you first began learning
your multiplication tables? I can, and it wasn't pretty. A classroom
of second graders struggling to memorize their "times threes" or
"times fours" and not really understanding why it was so important. Remember? It seemed like it was a never-ending series of
flash cards and practice tests and throughout the entire process
our teachers were telling us it was important to memorize the
multiplication tables because they were the foundation for all the
math we would learn in future. Without knowing basic multiplication, we would never be able to advance further in our understanding of arithmetic and mathematics.

In a similar way, good stewards need to understand that God's economy has its own principle of multiplication. If we ever want to move deeper into God's economy we need to memorize the principle of multiplication and begin applying it in our lives. That's one of the first steps on a Steward's Journey that leads us into experiencing exciting new dimensions of God's plans and how they can be accomplished through us. Just as important, it opens the door for us to observe God at work. There's no limit to what can be accomplished when we are willing to let God be God.

We've seen earlier on a Steward's Journey that generosity, not accumulation, is the key to prosperity, and the following verses serve as a reminder:

- "A miser in a hurry to get rich doesn't know that he'll end up broke." (Proverbs 28:22, MSG)
- "Blessed are those who are generous, because they feed the poor." (Proverbs 22:9, NLT)
- "A generous man will prosper; he who refreshes others will himself be refreshed." (Proverbs 11:25)
- "The world of the generous gets larger and larger; the world of the stingy gets smaller and smaller." (Proverbs 11:24, MSG)

Now let's look at more reasons why these proverbs are true, and why they describe what happens when stewards experience the multiplication factor by planting seeds of generosity.

It begins with a mind-set, and perhaps we can look to the modern world of business to help us understand how it works. In the business world it's not uncommon for two people to look at the

Notes:

same purchase from much different perspectives. Some view the purchase as an investment, while others consider it to be an expense. The first sees the purchase as a means of maximizing their profits in the long term, while the second focuses on the short-term reduction in his checking account.

Here's a real world illustration. Years ago my brother and I developed a product that helps florists safely transport their arrangements from the retail store to the customer's home or business. It solved a long-standing problem and prevented overturned arrangements and broken flowers that resulted in either higher costs if the florist remade the arrangement, or lower customer satisfaction if they delivered a damaged product. The interesting thing, though, is this. For those who were able to see the product as an investment, the decision to buy was a fairly easy one. They knew that spending some of their money in the short-term would bring more profits in return. Another group didn't see the purchase as an investment but as an expense. All they saw was money being spent with little to show for it. This group didn't buy because they couldn't see the long-term benefit. They held on to what they had and probably suffered financially in the long run.

Stewardship also has a mind-set. Will we be generous or stingy? It's our choice. Stewards consider their generosity to be an investment, not an expense. Paul says it this way: "Remember: A stingy planter gets a stingy crop; a lavish planter gets a lavish crop. I want each of you to take plenty of time to think it over, and make up your own mind what you will give. That will protect you against

Notes:

sob stories and arm-twisting. God loves it when the giver delights in the giving" (2 Corinthians 9:6-7, MSG). The more seeds we plant, the more crops will multiply to our account. It's really not very complicated. The key to the harvest isn't the size of our tractor or combine; the key to the harvest is the number of seeds we plant.

> The key to the harvest isn't the size of the tractor or combine; the key to the harvest is the number of seeds we plant.
> 🌿

Jesus said it this way in Luke 6:38, as reflected in three translations: "Give, and it will be given to you. A good measure, pressed down, shaken together and running over, will be poured into your lap. For with the measure you use, it will be measured to you." "If you give, you will receive. Your gift will return to you in full measure, pressed down, shaken together to make room for more, and running over. Whatever measure you use in giving—large or small—it will be used to measure what is given back to you" (NLT). "Give away your life; you'll find life given back, but not merely given back—given back with bonus and blessing. Giving, not getting, is the way. Generosity begets generosity" (MSG). It keeps coming back to generosity. How generous are we? How many seeds are we planting? How many opportunities are we opening for God to work through us? He's waiting.

Jesus told a story about sowing that illustrates how the multiplication factor works. He described a farmer scattering his seeds.

Notes:

Many of the seeds fell in the wrong places, but listen to what happened to the seeds that rooted in good soil: "Some seeds fell on fertile soil and produced a crop that was thirty, sixty, and even a hundred times as much as had been planted" (Matthew 13:8, NLT). Imagine a hundredfold return on your investment! In God's economy, when the investment is in His work and for His purposes, we don't have to merely imagine. God multiplies generous gifts to turn our imaginations into reality.

Here's another image I'd like us to consider. It's a situation most of us have been in ourselves at one time or another. We're standing on the shore of a pond or lake in the early morning, before the wind starts to blow. The water surface is like glass and there we stand, a stone in hand. You've been there, haven't you? It seems irresistible; we just have to toss the stone and watch the ripples fan out across the surface. I find it fascinating to watch how far the impact of a single stone can extend. The influence goes in all directions and keeps on until it finally loses its force. Change the picture just a little. What kid hasn't tried to skip the stone across the water's surface? A skipping stone impacts several places and generates a ripple effect wherever it touches. Similarly, a steward's generous giving has a multiplying ripple effect. As with the seed rooted in good soil, the return can be sometimes thirty, sometimes sixty, sometimes one hundredfold.

My wife and I are privileged to know a couple who have invested their lives in producing and planting basic teaching resources in the very fertile soil of the expanding church of

---

Notes:

Africa, Asia, Latin America, and other developing nations. Their work is called, appropriately enough, Hundredfold Ministries International (www.hundredfold.org). What amazing stories they have to tell. The Hundredfold Ministries model is something like this: an idea for a teaching article is written and distributed; a developing nation pastor receives the article and shares it with those in his care; church members or lay ministers hear the teaching and carry it to remote villages where they share it again and again. One teaching "seed," like a stone skipped across the water, impacts communities wherever it touches down. These seeds are life-giving to those who receive them. If you look at some of the stories on the Hundredfold Web site, you'll know what I mean. Hundredfold doesn't charge those in developing nations for the teaching resources it produces, it generously gives them at no charge. Hundredfold Ministries is much more than a name for this couple, it's a way of life. Hundredfold is a worthy ministry that produces a hundredfold return on any investments made in it.

Not all of the seed in Jesus' story fell on good soil. Those of us on a Steward's Journey need to look at the seed that fell on thorny ground. After telling the story, Jesus explained it for His followers. This is how Scripture describes the thorny ground: "The thorny ground represents those who hear and accept the Good News, but all too quickly the message is crowded out by the cares of this life and the lure of wealth, so no crop is produced" (Matthew 13:22, NLT). "The seed cast in the weeds is the person who hears the

Notes:

kingdom news, but weeds of worry and illusions about getting more and wanting everything under the sun strangle what was heard, and nothing comes of it" (Matthew 13:22, MSG). The *New International Version* refers to the "worries of this life and the deceitfulness of wealth." That sounds like the More War of chapter 3 to me and a warning for us to be careful. The choice is between a hundredfold return on the one hand or the worries and deceitfulness of life on the other.

There is another multiplication factor, especially in the American church, that we need to look at before moving on. In times of Extraordinary Giving (chapter 18) our giving can also have a positive impact on the giving of others. I've seen it happen again and again.

When local churches are in seasons where Extraordinary Giving is required, the challenge can often seem overwhelming and even impossible. Multiplication makes the impossible possible. Look at what faced Joshua and the nation of Israel as they prepared to enter the Promised Land. The Jordan River was at flood stage, not exactly the opportune time to cross. But Joshua identified twelve leaders, one from each tribe, to be the first to wade into the water. When they did, the impossible became possible as God was freed to do His work. The third chapter of Joshua records how the waters of the Jordan stopped flowing and allowed all the people to cross over as if it were dry land.

God sometimes calls leaders of His church today to step out in faith and begin a work that seems impossible. When they respond

Notes:

in obedience, though, something happens. The remaining people in the church see their leaders' faith and are inspired to action as well. The example of today's church leaders, just as David's captains and leaders in 1 Chronicles 29, can have a multiplying impact on the giving of others. Like ancient Israel, who saw the commitment of the twelve who stepped into an overflowing Jordan or who witnessed the response of leaders to David's challenge hundreds of years later, modern congregations can be inspired to give extraordinarily when they see their leaders set an example of Extraordinary Giving. The size of leadership gifts is multiplied many times over as other individuals and families commit to a season of Extraordinary Giving in order to achieve long-term ministry goals.

Occasionally we may hear of an opportunity for "matching gifts." We're told that an anonymous donor will match our contributions up to a certain amount. It's a great way to double the impact of our giving. A Steward's Journey, though, isn't about matching gifts up to a certain amount. A Steward's Journey is about multiplied gifts a hundredfold. If you haven't experienced the multiplication factor, think about doing it soon. There's absolutely nothing like watching God be God and multiplying our small gifts to accomplish His great plans. How? Be generous. Plant lots of seeds. Trade the cares of this life and the lure (and deceitfulness) of wealth for the hundredfold return. What have you got to lose?

Notes:

A Prayer for Your Day

Heavenly Father, take what we have and multiply it as only You can do. Take our small gifts and make the impossible possible. Take what we bring to You and skip it across the surface of Your church around the world, bringing a hundredfold return of blessing wherever it touches down. Show us the excitement that You have for us when we join where You are at work. Give us confidence to respond when You ask us to do what we think we can't. Use our example to inspire others to better stewardship on their own journeys. Thank You for letting us be a part of Your work. Amen.

❦

REFLECT & RESPOND

Imagine yourself standing on the shore of a mirror-smooth lake early in the morning, a flat stone in your hand. Imagine yourself skipping the stone across the lake's surface, ripples spreading outward from each touch point.

Now imagine having that multiplying influence in many places as a result of your good stewardship. Imagine God's blessing and good works spreading outward from each touch point.

Keep this image in your mind when you move to the next chapter and discover that no matter how much you can imagine, you can never imagine enough. God desires even more than the faithful steward can imagine.

SECTION FOUR

Reflections on the Journey

CHAPTER TWENTY-SIX

A Steward's Dreams

I can imagine a lot, but I can't imagine enough.

❧

*God can do anything, you know—far more than you could
ever imagine or guess or request in your wildest dreams!*
—EPHESIANS 3:20, MSG

I hope you'll forgive this personal example, but I think it helps
illustrate the responsibility that we have to be *stewards of our
dreams.*

In the last chapter I mentioned a floral industry product developed by my brother and myself. It's elegantly simple and probably could have been developed and marketed by literally
thousands of persons. But it wasn't. When we first began exhibit-
ing the product we repeatedly heard from those who saw it, "I had
that idea." We probably heard those exact words from hundreds
of people. Now, the fact is that they didn't have our idea, but they
had something close. Truthfully, the product we ended with was
not the same as the idea we began with. The major difference
between the idea that my brother and I had and the idea that
everyone else had is very simple: we did something about ours.
They didn't. We set out to make our idea—our dream—a reality

and in the process we created a profitable small business that continues to this day.

The God described in the Bible is a dream giver. He is the Creator of everything that exists (Colossians 1:16) and when He made mankind in His image, He gave us some of His creative characteristics. I believe He wants us to use our creativity more. I believe He gives us ideas—let's call them dreams—so that we can grow them into products and businesses that bring profits to us, resources to God's kingdom, and our acknowledgment that He was really the source behind both the idea and the success. I believe that because of verses like the one at the beginning of this chapter. Take time to explore what it means: "God can do anything, you know—far more than you could ever imagine or guess or request in your wildest dreams" (Ephesians 3:20, MSG). I don't know about you, but when I read this verse and then look at my reality I see a disconnect. It says that God can do far more than I could ever imagine, yet sometimes it seems like He's not active at all. What's going on?

Could it be that God is dealing with us like the master of the talents did with the servants that we read about in Matthew 25? Could it be that He has given us ideas, dreams, visions, plans, call them whatever you will, but that nothing is happening because in our fear, we've buried them just like the servant did? Could it be that the reason we don't see more of God at work is that He's waiting for us to be stewards over what He's already given us? Is it possible, and if so what can we do about it?

Notes:

The Bible describes people of faith as having a great inheritance, but if that's true, why does it appear that too many of us don't act like it? What are we missing? I wonder if we're missing action, like the people at the trade shows who had ideas but neglected to act on them. I wonder if we're guilty of not acting on what He's already called us to do. I wonder if the reason so little has been accomplished is because so little has been attempted. Do you ever think about that? Are there dreams in our minds and hearts that are waiting to be energized?

Teen Challenge didn't start as a large international organization; it started in God's heart. God shared His heart with David Wilkerson, David acted, and the rest is history. The same pattern has been repeated too many times to count throughout the centuries. But I don't think it has happened as often as God would like because somewhere in the process, things get bogged down, and I don't think it's God's fault. The problem is we haven't been very good stewards of the creativity He's given us.

Stop for a moment and think back in your own experience. Have you ever had a God-given dream to accomplish but after a while you walked away from it thinking it could never happen? If so, stop and take another look at what we've already learned on a Steward's Journey. If it was God's idea, regardless of the obstacles, not only does He want to see it done but He wants to see more accomplished than you can imagine. Frankly, that's a problem for me because I can imagine *a lot,* but the truth of the Scripture tells me that I can never imagine *enough.* Maybe it's time for each of

Notes:

us to examine our stewardship of dreams and ideas, take them out of cold storage, and put them into action. If that's the case, here are some thoughts that may help you move forward.

FEAR AND FAITH

Lots of things are never started because of the risk involved, but waiting to have all the answers has never been a viable option for a people who are called to live by faith. The element of faith keeps the steward dependent on God, and overcoming the fear and obstacles provides an opportunity to acknowledge God's central role when success is achieved. And don't forget this: Our faith is not as important as His faithfulness. If God places a dream in the steward's heart, He'll never abandon the steward or the dream. Paul said it this way: "The One who called you is completely dependable. If he said it, he'll do it!" (1 Thessalonians 5:24, MSG).

> **Our faith is not as important as His faithfulness.**
> ❦

FOLLY AND FAILURE

Maybe one of the reasons we're afraid to act on our dreams is that we've seen the folly and failure of others. Watching someone crash and burn isn't much of a confidence-builder, but neither should it paralyze us from being a good steward of the idea God has

Notes:

entrusted to us. Actually, witnessing the failure of others can be a great teacher because it forces us to discern whether our dream is rooted in faith or presumption. Presumption is a sure recipe for disaster, but the fact that others have presumed and failed shouldn't keep us from taking action ourselves when we sense confirmation that we're acting on God's behalf and not our own.

CONFIRMATION

"Make plans by seeking advice" (Proverbs 20:18). "Plans succeed through good counsel" (NLT). "Form your purpose by asking for counsel, then carry it out using all the help you can get" (MSG). Many failures have been avoided because people sought and listened to advice from wise and trusted counselors. None of us, after all, discerns perfectly. Sometimes it takes an objective yet spiritually attuned third party view to help us see what is all too obvious to those around us. Also, the older I get, the more confidence I have that God knows exactly what He's doing and the more confident I am that He wants unity within marriages before one spouse or the other takes action. Paul says in Philippians 2 that we should have the attitude of Christ. We wouldn't be told this if it weren't possible. More than that, as Paul writes in 1 Corinthians 2:16, "We have the mind of Christ." I think this means that He *wants* to share His mind with us. Where this becomes especially important is within marriages, when one spouse feels strongly but the other doesn't. What then? Wait! Pray

Notes:

for the mind of Christ for both spouses. What a feeling it is to hear the other say they're ready to move ahead or for both to agree to abandon a presumptive dream all because they've sensed God's will in the matter.

READ. PRAY. LISTEN. OBEY.

These are the guiding words from chapter 22, A Steward's Guide to Giving. They are also universally valuable when stewards consider anything God is asking of them. When we constantly are reading, praying, listening, and obeying it keeps us fresh in our relationship with Him. Who knows, maybe the mind that gets changed won't be your spouse's but yours! God works that way sometimes, but He can only get through to us if we listen.

Stewards are responsible for investing and maximizing their God-given dreams and goals. Just imagine what would happen if we all did our part. Just imagine what the world would be like if no steward ever had to wonder *What would have happened if....* Then remember that God's dreams are beyond our imagination! I wonder, what does He have in store for you?

Notes:

A Prayer for Your Day

*Heavenly Father, give us Your mind and give it gener-
ously! Teach us Your ways and train us to know them as
easily as we know our own. Help us to manage the ideas,
dreams, and plans that You share with us from time to
time. Cause us to act on them with wisdom and humility. Prevent us from boasting in success that belongs to
You. Then entrust us with more so that we can accomplish more. Keep us from inaction, regret, and what
might have been. Instead, show us the way to enter into
everything You have planned for us. Do this, Lord,
because it is a better way for us. Thank You. Amen.*

❧

REFLECT & RESPOND

Ask God to give you clear vision to see all that He has for you.

Has God dropped His dream into your heart, but it remains just a dream because you haven't taken action? Think about what you can do to change this.

Ask God to help you overcome fear that would keep you from His purpose.

Ask God to bring His provision into your vision, one step at a time, as you respond in obedience to His direction.

CHAPTER TWENTY-SEVEN

The Sincerest Form of Flattery

We honor God when we act as He does. God is a giver.

❧

I have set you an example that you
should do as I have done for you.
—JOHN 13:15

Genes are not the only thing we inherit from our parents. We also inherit their example. For better or worse, it's a powerful influence in shaping who we are and the type of people we will become.

Think about how this works out in our own culture. We see parents in immigrant families take on more than one job and work tremendously long hours not just to benefit themselves but to provide financial security and the promise of a better future for their children. In the process, these parents instill a real world appreciation of what hard work can accomplish. We witness military families constantly being uprooted and moved literally around the world and too often paying the terrible price of a loss of their soldier, sailor, airman, or marine. Yet a generation later, another family member takes the place of his or her fallen parent, perhaps continuing an unbroken chain of military service that has spanned many generations. The same is true for police or firemen or craftsmen that hand down their example and skills to their children, extending a long family tradition into a future generation. Sure, there's more than example at work here, but example plays a key role.

> Of all the gifts a steward can give to God, none is as meaningful as a life that conforms to the example of Christ.
>
> ❧

Years ago, a secretary at work called my attention to the power of example when she asked me to observe the interaction between two men. One was older and provided a stable role model for the younger, who'd had more than his share of problems on the wrong side of the law. She pointed out, though, that something significant was happening in the interaction between the two. Not only was the younger man changing his behavior for the good, he was also starting to *walk* and *act* like the older man. He wasn't mocking, he was imitating, and we've all heard the expression that imitation is the sincerest form of flattery. It was a fascinating observation and is an excellent illustration for us at this stage of a Steward's Journey. Why? Because of all of the gifts that a steward can give to God, there's none more meaningful than a life that conforms to the example Christ has given us. We honor God when we act as He does.

The context of Jesus' instruction in John 13:15 is sacrifice. Jesus had just completed washing the feet of His disciples in an

Notes:

act of humility and service. He gave of Himself and served others rather than expecting to be served, which He surely could have expected since He was equal with God. We already looked at Philippians 2 and the concept of Sacrificial Giving in chapter 17. Let's take another look, this time with the idea of listing the attributes of Jesus so we can follow His example.

"Your attitude should be the same that Christ Jesus had" (Philippians 2:5, NLT). We cannot imitate Christ unless we begin with our attitude. It's that simple. If we don't have Christ's attitude we'll end up hopelessly trying to follow a set of rigid, legalistic "Do's and Don'ts" and we'll fail miserably. Here's Paul's advice on the matter: "Let God transform you into a new person by changing the way you think. Then you will know what God wants you to do, and you will know how good and pleasing and perfect his will really is" (Romans 12:2, NLT). Notice that Paul says we have to change the way we think before we can know what God wants us to do. Attitude comes first.

"He did not demand and cling to his rights as God. He made himself nothing" (2:6-7, NLT). This is a hard one to work through in a culture that preaches entitlement as much as ours does. Why shouldn't we have a new car every two or three years? Why should we have to wait twenty years like our parents before we can have the same "stuff" they have? Why shouldn't we get a big raise even though the company earnings are down and jobs are in jeopardy? We live in a culture that elevates demands and clings to its rights, not the other way around like the example of Jesus. He made

---

Notes:

himself nothing. We try too hard to appear like we're something!

"He took the humble position of a slave ... he obediently humbled himself even further by dying a criminal's death on a cross" (Philippians 2:7-8, NLT). No one can follow this example of Jesus, but we can come to live our lives with a humility that honors His example. A few verses earlier Paul gives this counsel: "Don't be selfish; don't live to make a good impression on others. Be humble, thinking of others as better than yourself. Don't think only about your affairs, but be interested in others, too, and what they are doing" (Philippians 2:3-4, NLT). These are not easy things for many of us to do, at least they aren't for me, so let's review:

• Don't be selfish.

• Don't live to make a good impression on others.

• Be humble.

• Think of others as better than yourself.

• Don't think only about yourself.

• Be interested in others and in what they are doing.

It takes a new attitude and the mind of Christ to do this, and when I look at the list I'm reminded of Paul's comment in 1 Corinthians 15:31 that he dies daily. Because if we're really going to be successful in following Paul's advice, we have to do it *every day.* The good steward isn't perfect, but when he seeks to imitate Christ he does so *every day.* Don't be selfish *every day.* Be humble *every day.* Be interested in others *every day.* You get the idea. To imitate Christ is to give up our rights. *Every day.* That's not easy and that's why everything begins with attitude.

Notes:

When we imitate Christ we cannot help but become givers, because God is a giver. The most important example of this is found in John 3:16-17:

> This is how much God loved the world: He gave his Son, his one and only Son. And this is why: so that no one need be destroyed; by believing in him, anyone can have a whole and lasting life. God didn't go to all the trouble of sending his Son merely to point an accusing finger, telling the world how bad it was. He came to help, to put the world right again. (MSG)

There will never be another gift as valuable as this one, but the gift is only part of the story.

Paul Tournier, a Swiss psychiatrist, wrote a small book titled *The Meaning of Gifts.*[1] I've long since misplaced my copy of the book but one thing Dr. Tournier said has stayed with me. The true joy of the gift, he wrote, isn't in the giving of the gift but in seeing the gift used. We know that's true in our own experience. Joy doesn't come from watching a Christmas gift unwrapped and set aside. True joy comes in seeing the gift opened and used. True joy is watching someone take a gift and benefit from its use.

What does this mean for us? God has given us a gift that will never be equaled. But the full expression of that gift will never be fully realized until we open ourselves to it, accept it, and use it. The steward does. If you haven't, I hope you will. If you have, keep going!

Notes:

A Prayer for Your Day

Heavenly Father, help us to honor You by acknowledging
what You have done for us. Help us to have Your atti-
tude. Help us to consider others more than we consider
ourselves. Help us to become people known for our
humility and not our arrogance. Help us to follow Your
example in giving. Help us to see the value of the gift
You've given us and show us how to enter into its full
meaning and measure. May we bring joy to You when
we accept, and use daily, the gift of Your Son. Amen.

✾

REFLECT & RESPOND

Reflect on the stewardship example you are for others. Is your example something that others want to imitate?

On a scale of 1 (following a set of rigid "Do's and Don'ts") to 10 (having the attitude of Christ), where would you rate yourself and why?

How fully would you say that you experience the joy of God's gifts to you?

CHAPTER TWENTY-EIGHT

Understanding What's Important

Make the permanent your priority.

❧

The Kingdom of Heaven is like a treasure that a man discovered hidden in a field. In his excitement, he hid it again and sold everything he owned to get enough money to buy the field—and to get the treasure, too!
—MATTHEW 13:44, NLT

The realities of life have a way of changing our priorities. Many of us probably take our health for granted, until we feel a lump or the doctor sees a shadow on the x-ray. Things change then, and many things that were near the top of our priority list don't seem so important anymore. They may still be on the list but they don't get our attention the way they once did.

The book of Mark tells the story about a woman who had a hemorrhage for twelve years: "She had suffered a great deal under the care of many doctors and had spent all she had, yet instead of getting better she grew worse" (Mark 5:26). She spent everything she had and went from doctor to doctor seeking a cure. I know that some of you on a Steward's Journey know exactly how she felt because you're there, too. Whatever used to be a priority isn't one anymore.

Let's take that image one step further. Nothing seems to bring life into its proper focus as much as encounters with death. Don't close calls on the freeway or anxious moments awaiting biopsy results cause us to pause and rethink what's important? It seems that the more serious the crisis, the more likely priorities are to be reordered. After all, money isn't usually the central topic at a memorial service, life is, with all its memories and emotions. Which is more than enough reason for us to consider how we can be good stewards of our time and talent as well as our treasure.

> **Money isn't usually the central topic at a memorial service, life is.**
> ✦

Harry Chapin's song from the early '80s titled "Cat's in the Cradle" paints a great musical word picture about priorities. Maybe one of the reasons it became such a classic was its subject matter was so familiar to those who heard it. All of us have to make our own choices and determine what the proper balance of priorities is between parent and bread winner. For the father in Chapin's song it was earning a living that won out. That was his highest priority. It sent him on the road while his son took his first tentative steps. He was too far away to hear his son's first words. It caused him to prize making cash more than playing catch. Through it all his promise remained the same: later they'll get together, later they'll have a good time.

Notes:

Later never came. When the time finally arrived that dad wanted to spend time with his son, it was too late. His adult son now had priorities of his own and the door of opportunity to build a meaningful father-son bond was closed. The son had become just like his dad. It's a great song, but a really stinging message. A message of misplaced priorities.

Priorities changed. Once the most important thing was catching another plane, closing another deal, making more money. Planes, deals, and money are not permanent, though; they're means to an end, but not the end itself. The fortunate among us learn this lesson before it's too late. The fortunate are stewards of the important: things like faith, family, friendship, and wise financial management. I don't know how much Harry Chapin understood the truth of his lyrics. I hope he saw it clearly. Chapin died in a traffic accident when he was 38.

In the reference at the start of this chapter, Jesus uses a story to describe what the kingdom of heaven is like, and the bottom line of the story is this: Entering into the kingdom of heaven is worth more than anything we value on earth. The man in the story sold all he had to buy the field with the hidden treasure. When the man stumbled upon the hidden treasure, his priorities changed. Everything he'd accumulated in life up until that point didn't matter anymore. What mattered was the treasure in the field.

When we discover the true value and benefits of biblical stewardship, our priorities change too. Consumption becomes less important and investing in things that last moves up to the top of the

Notes:

list. Good stewardship means making the permanent our highest priority. How can we do that?

The investments we make in people are lasting investments. They should be high on our priority list. Married couples should invest whatever it takes for their marriage to thrive, not just survive. Parents should commit themselves to the proper training and development of their children. Moses gave this challenge to parents: "You must commit yourselves wholeheartedly to these commands I am giving you today. Repeat them again and again to your children. Talk about them when you are at home and when you are away on a journey, when you are lying down and when you are getting up again. Tie them to your hands as a reminder, and wear them on your forehead. Write them on the doorposts of your house and on your gates" (Deuteronomy 6:6-9, NLT). I'd say Moses considered this a priority, wouldn't you?

Stewards invest in the work of those doing God's work, because work done for God is work that lasts. Organizations like Teen Challenge and the Salvation Army touch and redeem lives. Stewards invest there. Other organizations bring food, shelter, or medical care in God's name to those who need it most. And along with providing these essentials of life, they also share the Good News of Jesus Christ. That's high priority work because it makes a permanent difference. Missionaries in America and around the world influence lives in ways we can never begin to imagine. They need our help, they need to become our priorities. Their work lasts.

Notes:

Priorities are personal and reordering our priorities is something every steward must do for themselves. We shouldn't be afraid of the process. Stewardship doesn't mean that we have to sell all we have and take perpetual vows of poverty. But it does mean that we should get our priorities straight and, as we'll see in the next chapter, make wise choices. There was a time in the Christian community when WWJD bracelets seemed to be everywhere. Good stewards don't have to wear the question on their wrist, as long as they are honestly asking it in their hearts. What Would Jesus Do? He would make the permanent His priority.

A Prayer for Your Day

Heavenly Father, there is so much activity that begs for
us to get involved. There is more than we can ever do.
Slow us down, Lord. Instruct us on what's important.
Direct us to those things that are close to Your heart and
then change our hearts to be passionate about them.
Amen.

🍂

REFLECT & RESPOND

List and rank the six or seven highest priority things in your life.

Do you think that God would reorder any of these priorities if He could and, if so, how would He rank them?

What specific things can you do to bring your priorities in line with God's?

CHAPTER TWENTY-NINE

Choices

Sominex or Serenity? Possessions or Possessors?

❦

Now listen! Today I am giving you a
choice between prosperity and disaster.
—DEUTERONOMY 30:15, NLT

How many choices have you already made today? If you're the mother of a young child or the owner of a small business and you're reading this chapter late at night, I'd say the chances are excellent you've made hundreds. Our lives are filled with choices, right? What meals to fix, how to resolve the disputes with the neighbor kids, how much to pay to get the top-notch mechanic, what to say at the teacher-parent conference, how much next year's advertising budget should be, where we can get the best value, what gift your mother-in-law will really like, which dress is the most slimming. Decisions, decisions, decisions. Doesn't it seem sometimes that life is one great big continuous choice? There isn't an area of our life that doesn't require us to choose.

The reality is that the choices we make shape the options that are available to us in the future. While it probably doesn't matter whether you fix tacos or meat loaf for dinner tonight, or buy file folders from Staples or Office Depot, there are choices that do matter. If you say the wrong thing to the neighbor or teacher, things can get a bit tense. And if you miscalculate the compensation package, the key employee you need to hire may turn down your offer.

Parents pray for their children to make wise choices because they understand that our choices have consequences. Consequences make great teachers because they provide feedback about the wisdom of the choices we make. When the consequences are obvious and immediate, we learn right away. It didn't take my body very long to tell me it didn't appreciate a dozen Krispy Kremes. I won't try that again no matter how tasty they look. There are positive consequences too. A smile often brings a smile in return. Excelling at work often leads to a raise or promotion, although this consequence usually isn't as obvious or immediate as most of us would like. Our own experiences have taught each of us the linkage between choice and consequence. Behavioral psychologists have their own terms to describe this connection, but I like to call it the law of natural consequences. It's inevitable; every choice comes with a consequence.

It's possible, though, to be shielded from the consequences. For example, a family of influence may use their power to keep their son out of legal trouble. The spouse of an alcoholic may make allowances for destructive behaviors and hide them from friends and co-workers. A teacher may extend the deadline for the completion of a major project. In virtually all instances, though,

Notes:

shielding only postpones the effect of consequences, it doesn't eliminate them. Eventually the consequences will be felt. Sooner or later, if we don't put gas in the tank, we're going to get stuck by the side of the road.

Unfortunately, our consumer culture likes to erect barriers that temporarily separate our financial choices from their natural consequences. Our credit-based culture depends on this blurring of the link between choices and consequences. Think about how things have changed in the relatively recent past. Only in the last twenty or thirty years have we been able to spend more than we earn. Before that, if we had the money we could purchase the item, and if we didn't we could put it on layaway. Those options, or doing without, were our choices. It wasn't that long ago that checks bounced if there wasn't enough money in our checking account to pay them. Checks were returned to merchants with "NSF" stamped on their front, and embarrassed consumers had to scramble to make them good. In a very short time period consumers experienced the consequences of writing checks without sufficient money in their bank accounts to make them good. Many of us can remember a list of these offenders posted behind the cash register at the local store. Wise people didn't want their name on that list because it meant they no longer had the choice of writing a check for their purchases. Bad choices brought limiting consequences.

Then along came something called "overdraft protection." The banks promoted overdraft protection as a valuable new service to

Notes:

the consumer that would help them out if they made a mistake in their checkbook register. In reality, it was the first block in a barrier that shields us from the consequences of our decisions. It wasn't long before overdraft protection turned into a line of credit, and we began using money we didn't have, not just to correct our short-term mistakes, but to satisfy our short-term desires. Unfortunately it also caused long-term problems.

Credit cards only made things worse. When they were first introduced, credit cards were issued by our local banks where we already had established accounts. In fact, it was usually a requirement to have a savings or checking account in order to get a credit card. Now we're flooded with credit card offers every day, and many consumers have credit accounts with several South Dakota finance companies. The 40 percent of American families that spend more than they earn use those credit lines to supplement their income. They use those credit lines to shield themselves from the consequences of their spending choices. For a while. Eventually something has to give. Eventually there won't be any more increases in the credit line or the equity in the house will be maxed out. What then? The consequences will be felt. We've come a long way from the layaway era, but are we better off?

The good steward makes good choices and avoids bad consequences. That's one of the primary lessons we've learned on our Steward's Journey.

Thousands of years ago Moses talked about choices as ancient Israel prepared to enter the Promised Land: "Today I am giving

Notes:

you a choice between prosperity and disaster. Today I have given you the choice between life and death, between blessings and curses. I call on heaven and earth to witness the choice you make. Oh, that you would choose life, and you and your descendants might live" (Deuteronomy 30:15,19, NLT).

Our choices today are essentially the same. We can choose:

- The prosperity that comes with wise financial choices or the disaster that follows foolish ones.
- Cultural consumerism or biblical stewardship.
- The blessings that are given to the good steward or the judgment that falls on the bad one.
- A generous or stingy lifestyle.
- Having possessions or being possessed by them.
- Investing in things that last or things that wear out.
- The serenity of contentment or the anxiety of needing more.
- Designer labels or generic brands that get the job done.

The list never ends.

It's time to stop and evaluate the consequences of our choices. Are we satisfied with where we are or concerned with where we're headed? Do we live with the satisfaction of being a good steward or the fear that time is running out and the consequences of our choices are coming due? Are our choices leading to prosperity or disaster?

Listen carefully. It's never too late to begin making right choices. It's never too late to honestly face the consequences. It's

Notes:

never too late to ask the owner of our resources how He wants us to manage them. It's never too late. *Never!*

That means it's not hopeless. Nothing ever is when God is involved. So if you've made your share of bad choices in the past, don't dwell on them. Stewardship doesn't live in the past, it maximizes the present. Regardless of where you are on a Steward's Journey, you have the promise of a better future. Consider these promises: "For I know the plans I have for you," says the LORD. "They are plans for good and not disaster, to give you a future and a hope" (Jeremiah 29:11, NLT). "Do not be afraid for I have ransomed you. I have called you by name; you are mine. When you go through deep waters and great trouble, I will be with you. When you go through rivers of difficulty, you will not drown! When you walk through the fire of oppression, you will not be burned up; the flames will not consume you" (Isaiah 43:1-2, NLT). I think these are God's promises for each of us. It's a consequence of choosing Him, of choosing the life of stewardship. It's our choice.

> **Stewardship doesn't live in the past, it maximizes the present.**
> ❦

Notes:

A Prayer for Your Day

Heavenly Father, help us to understand the choices that face us and show us the clear consequences of our decisions. Give us wisdom to see through the clutter that clamors for our attention and distracts us from a life of stewardship. Clear our minds to know what You want us to do and help us to make the wise choice. Amen.

REFLECT & RESPOND

Rate yourself on a scale of 1 to 10 in the following areas:
- 1 (cultural consumer) to 10 (biblical steward)
- 1 (disaster from foolish choices) to 10 (prosperity from wise choices)
- 1 (blessings) to 10 (judgment)
- 1 (generous) to 10 (stingy)
- 1 (own possessions) to 10 (possessions own you)
- 1 (investments that wear out) to 10 (investments that last)
- 1 (anxious) to 10 (content)

What important financial choices are you facing at this time? Reflect on the positive and negative consequences of these choices and ask God's help to choose wisely.

Every "Yes" has a "No." Think about times in your life when a choice you made limited your options to do other things. What did you learn then or can you learn now from those kinds of experiences?

CHAPTER THIRTY

A Companion for the Journey

It ain't over 'til it's over.

❧

There has never been the slightest doubt in my mind that
the God who started this great work in you would keep
at it and bring it to a flourishing finish.

—PHILIPPIANS 1:6, MSG

One of my lasting memories as a child was how my parents would linger at the curb after they drove one of my friends home. Just as soon as my friend was out of the car, I was ready to head for home, but my parents always waited. They never left until the front door opened and my friend was safely inside.

Something similar happened as I moved into young adulthood. I'll bet it happened to you, too. Whenever I'd take a trip of any length, my parents always gave me specific instructions, and you probably know what they were: "Call us when you get there." Remember? Sure you do, and you probably have asked, or will ask, the same thing of your children when the time comes. Why? Because our concern for those we love will not allow us to really rest until we know they've arrived safely at their destination.

I have good news for you as we begin this final chapter of *A Steward's Journey:* the God who began this great work in you is not done. He will keep at it and bring it to a flourishing finish! It doesn't get any better than that. In fact, He promises to be your companion as you continue your journey, because even though this book is at its end, your journey goes on. After all, it's never over until it's over, and our role as a steward lasts for a lifetime.

So I'd like to finish *A Steward's Journey* with a sampling of some promises God extends to you. I am absolutely convinced that, even though the process of becoming a biblical steward may involve some difficult decisions and changes in your life, with His help you will succeed.

Isn't it good to have a traveling companion? Especially one who knows the road ahead better than we do? If you've ever had the opportunity to travel overseas, to a non-English speaking country, you know that it can be an adventure. The look and sounds of words are strange to our unfamiliar eyes and ears. It's comforting to have a guide to navigate the unfamiliar territory, and God is that guide for all who take a Steward's Journey. Think about the following promises that are available to you.

Paul, in his letter to the church at Ephesus, wrote this: "When you believed in Christ, he identified you as his own by giving you the Holy Spirit, whom he promised long ago. The Spirit is God's guarantee that he will give us everything he promised and that he has purchased us to be his own people" (Ephesians 1:13-14, NLT).

Notes:

When we put our faith and trust in Christ, we are no longer alone. We have the Spirit of God in us to guide us and help us on the journey. And that same Spirit is also a reminder to us that God has invested Himself *in us* as a guarantee that His purposes will be completed in our lives.

When we look at it this way, the difficulties that we've talked about through *A Steward's Journey* become much more manageable. It's not impossible for us to realize financial freedom because nothing is impossible with God. We are not condemned to a life of anxiety and turmoil because Jesus has promised that He will give us a new kind of peace: "I am leaving you with a gift—peace of mind and heart. And the peace I give isn't like the peace the world gives. So don't be troubled or afraid" (John 14:27, NLT).

Here's how Eugene Peterson describes God's provision for us in his translation of Jesus' words in Matthew's gospel:

> Has anyone by fussing in front of the mirror ever gotten taller by so much as an inch? All this time and money wasted on fashion—do you think it makes that much difference? Instead of looking at the fashions, walk out into the fields and look at the wildflowers. They never primp or shop, but have you ever seen color and design quite like it? The ten best-dressed men and women in the country look shabby alongside them. If God gives such attention to the appearance of the wildflowers—most of which are never even seen—don't you think he'll attend to you, take pride in you, do his best for you? What I'm trying to

Notes:

do here is to get you to relax, to not be so preoccupied with getting, so you can respond to God's giving. People who don't know God and the way he works fuss over these things, but you know both God and how he works. Steep your life in God-reality, God-initiatives, God-provisions. Don't worry about missing out. You'll find all your everyday human concerns will be met. (Matthew 6:27-33, MSG)

I think you could make a pretty strong case that a person can be considered rich if they've said good-bye to anxiety, never missed out, and have all of their everyday concerns met. What about you?

Just a few more paragraphs and this chapter will close, and a new chapter in your life will open. Thinking about that has sent my mind back to something that was said at the beginning of *A Steward's Journey*:

Another thing about journeys. Sometimes our most exciting and memorable ones are those where we end up in unexpected places. Places where, once we arrive, we discover many magnificent things we would have missed had we stayed on the main road.

The thought occurs to me, at the end of our journey together, that some of you are now at that unexpected place. You may have started *A Steward's Journey* for any one of a hundred reasons, but asking God to be your companion in life was not among them.

Notes:

Then, somewhere in the last thirty days, you made the discovery that life was too short and you had too much to lose to continue ordering your personal and financial affairs the way you have in the past. The way of the steward, perhaps a little frightening at first, became more and more attractive with each passing day until now, at the end, you've decided that this should not be the end of your Steward's Journey, but the beginning. You'd like the steward's way to be your way. You'd like to have a new companion join you as you continue life's journey. But you're not sure how.

Each day we've ended our time together with a prayer and a Reflect and Respond exercise, giving you the opportunity to interact with the information we've discussed. Today that interaction describes how you can make the way of the steward the way of your life, starting now. If God, in the form of His only Son Jesus, is not yet your life's companion, you can change that today.

A Prayer for Your Day

Heavenly Father, I don't understand everything that You have planned for me but I invite You to show me Your way. I want to be a faithful steward. I want someday to hear You say "Well done!" I know that I can't do this alone, I need Your help. Create a desire in me to follow Your plan for my life. Change my heart. Change my priorities. Change me. Amen.

REFLECT & RESPOND

If you would like to become a better steward of the resources God has entrusted to your care, ask Him for help. He is worthy of your trust. Think about it.

If you would like to invite God to be your companion for the rest of your life's journey, ask Him to be. It's as simple as this:

- Acknowledge Him as a God who is perfect in all ways.
- Confess the fact that you do not measure up to His perfection, a condition the Bible labels sin.
- Admit there is nothing you can do on your own to bridge the gap between God's perfection and your imperfection.
- Accept the historical fact that Jesus, the Son of God, was sent to earth to bridge this gap for us.
- Ask Jesus to be your companion, the guide who will direct you into a life of blessing and satisfaction.

Nothing you will ever do compares in importance to making the choice to invite God into your life. If this is something you would like to do, pray the following prayer. You don't have to understand everything about the road ahead, He'll show you the way. And be sure to tell your pastor about the decision you've made!

A Prayer for the Rest of Your Life

Heavenly Father, I believe that You are there. I'm sorry that my imperfections, what Your Word calls sins, have kept me away from knowing You, but I accept the sacrifice that Jesus made to bring me into Your presence. That is where I want to be. I invite You into my life. I invite You to change me into the person You've always planned for me to be. I invite You to be the Lord of my life, and I will be your steward. Amen.

❦

Notes

Chapter 5

1. Howard Dayton, *Your Money Counts* (Wheaton, IL: Tyndale House, 1997).

Chapter 6

1. Thomas J. Stanley and William D. Danko, *The Millionaire Next Door* (New York: Pocket Books, 1996).

Chapter 7

1. Rick Warren, *The Purpose Driven Life* (Grand Rapids, MI: Zondervan, 2002).

Chapter 9

1. Personal correspondence with the author.
2. Unpublished. Personal knowledge of the author.
3. Unpublished. Personal knowledge of the author.

Chapter 11

1. Henry T. Blackaby and Claude V. King, *Experiencing God* (Nashville: LifeWay Press, 1990).
2. E. M. Clark, *How to Be Happy Giving Your Money Away* (Springfield, MO: Clark, 1996).
3. George Muller, *The Autobiography of George Muller* (Kensington, PA: Whitaker House, 1984).

Chapter 21

1. Unpublished. Personal knowledge of the author.

Chapter 22

1. Carol Cymbala, *He's Been Faithful* (Grand Rapids, MI: Zondervan, 2001).

Chapter 23

1. Francis Schaeffer, *How Should We Then Live?* (Wheaton, IL: Crossway Books, 1976).

Chapter 27

1. Paul Tournier, *The Meaning of Gifts* (Louisville, KY: John Knox Press, 1968).